Absentee Parent Left Behind Child

A Discussion Guide for Parents

SCOTT LUPER, MA

Printed by Createspace
Charleston, South Carolina

Copyright © 2011 R S Luper

LCCN: 2011962100

Paperback:	ISBN: 1460975359
Paperback:	ISBN-13: 978-1460975350
E-Book:	ISBN-13: 978-1452411897
Spanish Edition:	ISBN: 1467960454
Spanish Edition:	ISBN-13: 978-1467960458
Large Print Edition:	ISBN: 1461144280
Large Print Edition:	ISBN-13: 978-1461144281

DEDICATION

To those left to raise the child of an absentee parent
and every precious child left to question why.

CONTENTS

Acknowledgments   I

1   Introduction   1

2   What's going through my child's head?   9

3   How do I minimize potential issues?   15

4   The first step   21

5   What should I tell my child?   31

6   When should I tell my child?   41

7   How should I tell my child?   55

8   Where should I tell my child?   61

9   The process   67

10   The pitfalls   71

11   Blaming the child   75

12   Forcing the issue   83

13	Answering more than they ask	89
14	Telling before they're ready	95
15	Being overly critical	101
16	Sugar coating or creating martyrs	109
17	Lying	115
18	Helping my child	125
19	What else should I know?	137
20	Conclusion	141
	Appendix A	145
	Appendix B	147
	Appendix C	149
	About the author	150

ACKNOWLEDGMENTS

While it's impossible to name everyone who contributed to this project, some must be mentioned:

My wife Vanessa and our sons Preston and Hudson. My father Randy, mother Karen, in-laws Bea and Emilio, sister Kristina and brother Kevin

Kathy Brinkley, Jeff Winn, Martha Fuller, Martha Grammer, Melinda Veatch, Steve Jester, Dr. Maribel Diaz-Esquivel

Dr. Pam Garcy, Dr. Sandra K Young – Whigham, Dr. Pat Love, Dr. Savita Abrahams, Dr. Randy Nobblitt, Dr. Brenda Wall, Dr. Marilynn Kissinger, Dr. Susan Justitz, Dr. Peggy Auguste, Dr. Michael Leach, Dr. Don Clements, Dr. Abby Calisch, Dr. Tim Branaman, Dr. Azadeh Ajami

All the professors I've had the privilege to study under and the students I've had the honor to study with.

Surraine Krause and Kay Lynn Bole

INTRODUCTION

Single parents, grandparents, and caregivers in this situation dread the day their child turns and asks the question. If you're reading this book, you know the question. Some plan for it from the moment one or both parents step out of the child's life.

It could come in the form of a question like, "Do I have a daddy?" or "Where's my Mama?" Maybe the child will ask, "How come it's just you and me?" It could come in a myriad of forms but whatever the question; the sentiment's the same. Something's different about me and I don't understand why.

This even extends to the children of parents who remarry. Children, aware of an absentee parent, may have a different set of issues and considerations. However, just like the questions of the single parent child, there's a feeling something about them is different from their classmates and friends.

An increasing number of kids in today's society are facing the reality that something's different about their situation. As the parent or guardian, you're left to answer the onslaught of questions and relational issues left in a parent's absence.

These can bring some of the most awkward, unpleasant moments a parent or guardian will endure, not to mention the significant other who has taken the parenting role left otherwise vacant. However, with the right approach, these moments can bring parent and child closer than you might imagine.

How do you, as a single or remarried parent (or grandparent or guardian for that matter) deal with the questions and realizations that something's different? How do you turn these situations into moments of warmth and bonding? That's why you're here. In fact, that's why I'm here. I've personally researched and undergone the process of writing this as much for myself and my family as I have for you.

I too have been a single parent. I'm now a remarried parent as well as a person with a master degree in clinical psychology and I have something to admit to you. Even with all my training and preparation for the moment described above, I was ill-prepared when the questions started coming. That's why I set out to discover not only the right way to tell a child about an absentee parent but also and equally important, the most common pitfalls to avoid in this situation.

After going through the turmoil of asking friends, and friends of friends, and strangers from all walks of life in this situation, I decided to put my discoveries down on paper in the hopes that you, having a child in similar circumstances, would benefit from my inquiries. This book was written, not only as a preparation tool for those in this situation, but also as a quick reference to revisit as the inevitable approaches.

I wrote this book for women and men raising children by themselves or with significant others who are not the absentee birth parent. As well as grandparents and other relatives and friends who find themselves in this unenviable position: caregiver to an absentee parent's child.

The ranks of parents and caregivers of these children have grown dramatically in recent decades. That being said, no matter how commonplace the situation it feels personal, isolating, and completely unique to the person fielding the questions.

I've used the phrase "absentee parent" several times and the term is somewhat intuitive, but the meaning of words is important. I want to ensure we all envision the same person when you see the phrase "absentee parent".

3

My definition of absentee parent is a birth parent not playing an active, continuous role in their child's life. The title is assigned to, or defined by, the parent's actions rather than circumstances or position. If they don't make a personal impact on their child's daily life, a parent may be labeled absentee.

Some would say their significant other or spouse happens to be a solider at war or a person traveling on business to support their family. Those situations can be very different depending on the parent's behavior in their absence, and by the way, do not require the use of this book.

A person who is absent solely to support their family writes letters or emails. They call on a frequent basis. These parents live with the child or visit regularly when not otherwise detained. You'll find children in this situation ask completely different questions.

Others might ask about the parent who only has visitation. This again is a situation, different from absenteeism. If the parent takes their regular visitation and has contact with their child between visits, they aren't by definition absentee. There are a great many parents responsibly co-parenting children with an estranged spouse or former partner. For those parents, this book isn't a condemnation; it's also not applicable to such situations.

I've spoken not only with single parents, parents with significant others, and grandparents and friends in our situation, but also with several absentee parents who have found themselves alienated from their child's life for any of a number of reasons. This was done as much to seek insight into my own child's situation, as it was for the purposes of this book.

I found few who didn't at least think of their child on a regular basis. The majority of parents interviewed, who were not absent due to work related issues, cited fear as their number one reason for absence. They stated they feared either rejection from the child, their own inabilities as a parent, or the awkwardness they might encounter with the other parent. It was also noted the longer a parent goes without contact with their child, the greater the fear and anxiety about re entering their life.

Of course there are a percentage of absentee parents who find themselves either too busy with their current lives or too immature to rise to the challenge of raising children. When a caregiver encounters absentee parents of this nature, it's merciful they don't play an active role in the child's life.

Some of those polled sighted a fear of judgment from the child over their absence, as well as a fear the child had been told untruths that might render the relationship irreconcilable.

For the sake of clarification, I don't ever encourage the above listed behavior. Negative discussion about the other parent only hurts the child and serves no positive end, other than making the parent feel better, momentarily. Such behavior is referred to as Parental Alienation Syndrome. Beyond the harm to the child, this behavior's not looked upon kindly in court cases, not to mention exceedingly easy to prove.

As an odd side note, a surprising percentage of absentee parents stated they feel the responsibility lies with the primary caregiver to initiate contact between themselves and their child. They further expressed a feeling that the primary caregiver was simply not doing a good job facilitating contact between the absentee parent and their child.

I couldn't disagree more. The responsibility of contact lies with the absentee parent. If you are comfortable acting as facilitator, please do. I'd personally find that a difficult role to fill.

Several single mothers have asked why this book isn't entitled, "Discussing an Absentee Father with Your Child". Twenty five years ago single fatherhood might have been an anomaly sufficient to not even require mentioning. However, this is no longer the case.

Increasing numbers of men find themselves filling the role of primary caregiver. I reflect this change, in the same way Mother's

Day Out programs nationwide are opting to change their names to Parent's Day Out. In this day and age, absenteeism doesn't discriminate gender, race, religion, or creed. Children are being left with mothers, fathers, grandparents, relatives and friends in all sectors of society.

In the course of this book, you should gain an idea of what to expect from your child and what's going on in their growing minds when they ask questions about their absentee parent. You'll receive the who, what, when, where, how, and why you should tell your child about their absentee parent.

Beyond that, the book details the seven most common pitfalls to avoid when discussing an absentee parent with your child. The book ends with a discussion about helping your child avoid the same scenario and other helpful ideas for your journey.

What this book won't do is offer a single heading or silver bullet that definitively puts a stop to questions about an absentee parent or offer a perfect singular list of questions with perfect responses. Each child is different, as is each and every style of parenting and home environment. These differences make for a unique situation between you and your child.

I can tell you that honest, open communication is the most important trait you'll rely on when answering questions about your child's absentee parent. An amazing added benefit of this experience is that it should help foster a healthier, more loving relationship with your child. Even if you already share a strong relationship, you'll see improvements over time after integrating these simple principles into your current parenting plan.

As for this books format, it's laid out in a manner which addresses some of the most important questions you may have when discussing your child's absentee parent. Throughout the process you'll learn what to say, how to say it, when to say it, and where it should be said. Each is so intertwined with the topic of why you should tell your child about their absentee parent, I've laced the subject throughout each chapter of this book.

The second half includes chapters on each of the most common pitfalls a parent might encounter, along with a liberal dose of examples and reasons to avoid each pitfall.

That being said, this book is an important step in learning the appropriate way to react to, and interact with, your child, and the questions they'll ask about their absentee parent. You'll be better prepared than most, because you're taking this time to do the necessary work. I wish you the best on this journey and hope for the most positive outcome possible for everyone involved.

WHAT'S GOING THROUGH
MY CHILDS' HEAD?

There are so many times as a parent, or guardian, you have the opportunity to ask, "What's going through my child's head?" For instance, when they decide the family-get-together is the perfect place to institute something they like to call "I'm a superhero and you're not", which of course includes wearing their Underoos on the outside of their shorts and Moms robe as a cape. When they decide to bring a live frog to school in their backpack so... "Hoppy can see what kindergarten's really like". There are a multitude of times from coloring on walls to eating a bug, when you have the chance to ask yourself, "What's going through my child's head?"

Honestly I have no insight into bug eating, frog trafficking, or superhero time, but I can tell you how a child's mind generally works at a certain age. I can tell you why they're asking, what they're asking, and the way they're asking it. I can tell you what to look for along the way, to predict the next series of questions.

Several groups of scientists and researchers have looked at child temperament through a number of studies. Each study generally found that most children fall into one of three categories, Easy, Difficult, and Slow to Warm.

The easy kids can handle most things and flow with the changes. Slow to warm kids are similar to easy kids, but they're a little more wary of strangers – not a bad quality in the opinion of most parents. The difficult kids are well, difficult. They aren't easy going. They tend to fight and get mad easily. They cry more and they do it longer. The studies determined that, while most kids fall into one of these three categories, more than a third of children don't fall into any category. Each child presents with their own challenges, no matter which of the four captions they fall under.

The reason I tell you this is because your child's temperament plays a role in their perception of their situation. There are also environmental factors, outside forces, that impact a child. These factors and many more, like genetics, prenatal environment, stress, and reactivity have an impact on how your child perceives their situation.

One of the largest environmental factors is living situation. Is it stable or unstable, meaning does the household consist of you, your child, and maybe grandparents or some other constant adult? Or is the house a revolving door for relatives and friends who come in and out of the child's life?

Another factor affecting children is the matter of "when" the parent became absent and how absent they are. It could be the absentee parent was actively in the picture at some point and slowly lessened their involvement. It could be the absentee parent comes around sporadically and unpredictably. Still other absentee parents play an active role for a time, only to abruptly cease contact for one reason or another.

In my child's case, the visits grew fewer and fewer over the first year of his life, ending around his first birthday. He had no concept of the word "mother" until he was nearly three years old. In our case, however I married my wife just after his fifth birthday. Consequently he has no memories prior to his intact family; although he is aware he has a birth parent separate from his mom, my wife.

Without regard to the factors listed above, children start asking questions when they reach three to five years of age. The questions will begin very simple and vague and become more specific, and consequently more difficult to answer, as your child grows and gains more awareness of their situation.

Until three to five years of age, children focus on the rudiments of day-to-day life. They're absorbed in the mechanics of walking, talking, facial recognition of family members and tasks we as adults take for granted on a daily basis.

Once they piece together an impressive vocabulary, start to assemble full sentences and carry on conversations with you, your child will start making determinations about the world around them and their place in it. For better or worse, they'll draw on the building blocks and parental modeling they have available to make these determinations. As they're introduced to more experiences, they'll continue to grow intellectually and with this growth comes more realizations, which inevitably spark more questions.

In my child's case, he thought all kids had a dad, a grandma, and a granddad. Children see their situation as the norm and won't change that opinion until they determine otherwise based on some outside stimuli.

For him, it wasn't until he started paying attention in his Parent's Day Out program that he noticed the other kids had grandmas like he did, but they called them "Mama". To him, "Mama" was the name of every woman between 15 and 60. This was obviously an issue I had to address.

Eventually, as children progress through school they learn more and gain the ability to think abstractly. As this happens, there will be even more questions, with even more difficult answers. This may sound overwhelming but it's nothing to worry about. So long as you follow the steps in this book you'll do well.

You may ask why that is. The steps show you how to build on each question, making each answer only slightly more difficult than the last. Just as your child will progress in school from simple addition to algebra to calculus and trigonometry, their questions will progress on a continuum as well. Allow them to be where they are on that continuum. You wouldn't expect your four year old to work quantum physics theorems or throw a perfect slider. In this same way you can't expect them to understand a force fed story of their absentee parent. Allow them the time they need. It's necessary for their processing of the event.

In my child's case, he justified his situation using Walt Disney cartoons. He noticed Mickey Mouse didn't have a mother, neither did Minnie Mouse. Hewey, Louie, and Dewey didn't have a mother but Uncle Donald did take care of them. Goofy's son Max didn't have a mother either. He was raised by Goofy. The same was true for the Little Mermaid and Belle in Beauty and the Beast.

He used the building blocks he had in front of him to make determinations about his own surroundings. Your child will no doubt do the same. They'll probably make different correlations than this Disney example, but they'll make correlations that are important for them, none the less.

Pay attention for these moments of clarity, they provide perfect opportunities to ask your child if they have any questions. If they don't, as my child didn't in the beginning, don't force the issue. They're verbalizing their thought processes, which is exactly what you want. Be waiting for their questions about the absentee parent. They'll come.

HOW DO I MINIMIZE POTENTIAL ISSUES?

In general, the absence of a parent can manifest itself in a number of insecurities and issues in a child. Many children face abandonment concerns at some point in their childhood or adolescence. The absence of a parent can present in the form of anxiety, self esteem issues or a host of other, equally serious, fears and social disorders.

No one wants their child to face these or a multitude of other fears and concerns. The golden question is how do I accommodate for, and minimize, the possible issues? Be there for your child. I know it sounds simple, but it's completely true.

Your child stands an increased chance of facing these issues, and the only way to combat them is for your child to know with exacting certainty that you're with them, every step of the way. I

15

know a good portion of those reading this book are thinking the word, "Duh".

It sounds simplistic, but think about this. How much time do you spend away from your child due to work? How much time do you spend on church, school, or social activities? Now think about the time you're in the same house, but in separate rooms, or even the same room doing different things.

When possible, set aside time daily to focus solely on your child. That means no cell phone calls or reading, no talking to friends or watching TV. Let your child know it's their time. They are the most important thing in the world to you and this time is theirs.

Of course, the preceding wasn't said to upset anyone or question their commitment. I know you're busy and I know you're doing everything you can. I believe your child means the world to you. If they didn't, you wouldn't be reading this book and worrying about how to answer these questions in the best way possible. What I am saying is that being cognizant of the time you have with your child, as well as being aware of what you do with that time, will have an amazing impact and will make an incalculable difference.

For me it's the time he and I spend in the morning getting him ready for school. My son, my wife, and I also spend at least thirty minutes together playing at the park or watching an episode of some cartoon. We eat dinner together, and then later in the evening we go over his homework. My wife and I finish the day by taking turns reading him a story before bedtime.

This may sound like a lot of time and energy. However, when put into the context of a normal day, it's really not. I can assure you though, that time makes all the difference in the world. Adding it up in my head, it comes out to between an hour and a half and two hours a day.

You don't have to do all the activities mentioned. You don't have to do any of them. That's our routine because it works for us. It doesn't have to be yours. What is important is that you spend as much time as you can and spend it focusing solely on them and their little lives.

During this time you have the opportunity to tell them how special they are. Tell them they're smart and pretty. Tell them how proud you are of them and above all tell them you love them.

I've come to notice, especially during finals week, my child lets me know if he hasn't had his time with me. He'll sit in my lap and ask me to hold him or he'll ask me to watch something with him. When that happens, I come to a stopping point and give him the time he deserves.

You're all your child has. They need to know you're there, that you love them and that you're proud of the person they're becoming. This reinforcement is essential. As I've said before, I don't mean for anyone to quit their job and spend their days and nights hovering over their children. This is both impractical and unreasonable, for everyone involved. I'm advocating mindfulness of the time you have available to you and how you're spending it.

With the issues and concerns listed above and the time you have to commit to your child, am I saying a child is always better off with both parents? No, of course not. If a child is endangered or in some way neglected, it's obviously not a better scenario for anyone involved. If the parent introduces dangerous activities or people, they shouldn't be inflicted on the child either. Let's face it, there's a reason they're no longer in your life.

Kids are not better off with two parents who stay together, only to spend every waking moment fighting. In several cases the chaos introduced by an absentee parent, forced back into a child's life, makes the parents absence favorable. Of course my opinions should never take the place of your own legal counsel or personal convictions.

That being said, I do believe if an agreement can be reached between the adults in the child's life that allows them to co-parent and act in the best interest of the child, that kid will be better off in the long run than one who witnesses constant abuse or has no adult, modeling appropriate behavior in place of the absentee parent. As mentioned before, these positions aren't maintained by absentee parents, but rather by a person who's been there for the child and made concerted efforts throughout their life.

This book helps you talk to your child about a parent who's not in the picture. This causes statements about co-parenting or two singular, active parents to have little relevance in this situation. If a parent is an active part of their child's life, this book will only serve to provide a window into the experiences of myself and others.

Some might ask, "What if my child's different than the ones listed in the book?" Your child won't be exactly like the children in this book. They certainly won't be exactly like my child, outside of examples pertaining to him. But, intricacies aside, children will, for the most part, follow the steps I'll address in coming chapters. They may reach the milestones in their own time, but they will almost invariably reach them. Some children may ask their questions all at once, others may wait until their thirties.

These differences are attributed to the minutia that makes every child different, from upbringing to genetics to experiences. It's important to remember, the questions will come and when they do, you'll know how to answer and what to say. That being said, in the next chapter we'll discuss a parents vantage point and frame of reference.

THE FIRST STEP

Before discussing anything else, it's important to examine your vantage point as caregiver. When asked what their focus is, parents invariably say it's their child, which makes sense.

However, when questioned further, a large percentage of these same parents speak mainly about the absentee parent. They understandably discuss the ways they were wronged by the absentee parent and how difficult parenting is since the other person's departure.

This mindset puts the parent's focus and energy in the wrong place. It could also cause issues for the child. Therefore it's impossible to move forward responsibly without looking at your vantage point as a parent/caregiver. I realize some might say I haven't explained their point of reference.

I can't, and would never pretend to, understand anyone else's experiences. What I do know is the tendencies of this process and the tendencies of a great many I've spoken with in our situation. With that said, open your mind to the possibility it's time to do some serious work. Keep in mind you're doing this for the health and well being of your child, which makes the work well worth the time and energy.

I realize how difficult it can be to let go of the emotion you may be harboring for the absentee parent. I can honestly say I took these same steps and did my own work while personally going through this process, but I can't think of a person more worthy of the time and effort than my little one. For you, I'm certain there's no one more worthy than your child.

Others may say, "That has nothing to do with me. I'm already remarried," or "I've found someone else. I've moved on. They don't even come into the equation". It's entirely possible to feel that way, but the absentee parent does hold a place in the equation. It's important your child have the opportunity to know they have an absentee parent and that they feel safe in asking questions about them. Keep the focus on your child and not the opportunity to erase any record of the absentee parent.

Some parents I've interviewed have revealed that, in the absence of the other parent, they have worked harder to foster a belief in the child that the new significant other is taking the place of the absentee parent. This is a dangerous position to put yourself and your child in. While the other person may assume the role of a parent and may even move into a position of comfort with the child where it would seem normal to have the child call them Mom or Dad, I'd make a point of caution.

I agree there are cases where a man or woman can seamlessly take up the mantle left vacant by the absentee parent. In fact that's the situation I've found myself in. I can happily say my wife assumed all the duties left bare by my son's absentee parent to the point he does see her as his mother. And for all intents and purposes, she is. But while he looks to my wife for comfort, safety and love as any child would, he's still aware of the fact he has a birth mother who is different from my wife. It's important that children are privy to information concerning their birth parent.

This can easily come from the significant other who might occasionally mention something to the effect of, "I'm so glad I chose you. You're the most amazing little girl/boy in the world". Or you could possibly say, "Even though (Significant Other) wasn't with us when you were born, I'm so glad we found them for us". I don't believe, in a case such as this, it would even be inappropriate to say, "(Significant Other) may not be your birth mother/father, but they are a great Mama/Daddy". Another good statement might be, "If you have any questions about your birth parent, please come to me and ask. I'm happy to answer any questions. I want you to have all the information you want".

Any of these will get the point across – there is an absentee parent who's not in the picture. There is a person besides their primary caregiver and that knowledge doesn't change how much they love or care for you. Any mindset that goes against this openness and frankness can only hope to backfire. It always will, but we'll discuss that at further length in future chapters.

Whenever thinking about how important this process is to the overall mental health and happiness of your child, I'm reminded of a story about a friend. This mother found herself agitated with her six year old son over something he'd done. She got down on his level to admonish him and asked, "What are you doing, little man? Do you think you're the center of the universe?" The little boy looked at her sincerely and replied, "I'm the center of your universe. That's why you call me your son (sun)".

I love that story because it gets to the heart of the situation. That little boy displayed wisdom beyond his years and hit the nail on the head.

Whether you have a boy, a girl, or some combination of multiple kids, your child/children are the center of your universe. Very few parents would argue this statement. That being said, it's still difficult to make that important move from devoting time and energy to the parent who isn't in the picture, to removing the emotion and reallocating your efforts. The vast majority of parents are unaware they devote so much energy and emotion to the absentee parent. For most it's a scary process, letting go of such strong emotions. But how do you make that change?

A move this significant is referred to as a paradigm shift, meaning you have to fundamentally change your basic assumptions about a subject. It can also be thought of as the way you think. I wish I could say paradigm shifts were easy, common transformations. Unfortunately nothing's farther from the truth. If paradigm shifts were easy, there'd be no suffering due to alcoholism or other forms of substance abuse. There'd be no divorces or need for diet programs. Paradigm shifts are hard to make, but they're also essential in order for this, or any other worthwhile change to take hold.

I'm reminded of an example of how difficult it can be to make a paradigm shift. There was a series of studies done several years ago that asked chain smokers how likely they were to die of lung cancer. The vast majority of participants in these studies stated a much higher likelihood they would die of some tobacco related disease or complication than the actual national averages would indicate. What does this tell us? Smokers believe smoking to be more deadly than it statistically is, but even with this inflated information they still have difficulty stopping.

I don't say any of this to scare you, just the opposite in fact. I'm giving you this information to prepare you. So you'll be ready and successful in taking the necessary steps. Remember you have motivation to help maintain accountability while you make this change. Your child's happy, adoring face serves as a reminder of the change you're working towards. With that in mind, you can make that shift in focus, from the hurt and pain the absentee parent caused, to the love and care you have for your little one.

Some may wonder what makes this specific shift so difficult. An outsider might say, "What's the big deal? You say you don't like them. You complain about them. How could it be that difficult?" I can assure you, however, it is a big deal, and here's why. Anger and frustration can be powerful emotions. You feel righteous in your indignation for the one who isn't there to share in the milestones and challenges of childrearing. It's difficult to give up such a powerful emotion, even if it is negative and possibly destructive.

On the same token, giving up such strong emotion can be frightening and anxiety provoking. You might feel naked or vulnerable without such a powerful emotion. You also realize once you try to change your way of thinking, just how much time and energy is expended focusing on that person. This can be a difficult emotion to deal with as well; understanding how much time, emotional energy and possibly even turmoil is spent on the person who isn't there.

So now that you're sufficiently aware, I can tell you there is a way to make this change. Some say it takes twenty one to thirty days to develop a habit, be it good or bad. So just like you learned the habit of devoting energy and emotion to the person who isn't there, it should take roughly three to four full weeks of serious work to change the habit of anger to a more positive one of love and acceptance towards your child. How do you go about that?

The method is different for different people. I hesitate to give you a specific plan because what works for one person won't necessarily work for another. I'd rather you find your own method than get discouraged when you try one that's not tailored for you. I can give you the general outline to follow, with you making the necessary changes to ensure your success.

The general approach to shifting your habit is to decide ahead of time what positive thought you will replace the negative thought with. Whether it's the thought of your child or a self affirming statement, the method needs to consistently transfer your thought from the negative to the positive.

That's not to say you're never allowed to have those thoughts again. Such a claim would be setting you up for a losing proposition. It would be akin to asking you not to think about a purple monkey. Whatever you do for the next sixty seconds, don't think about a purple monkey. I'll bet I can guess what you're thinking about.

You'll have those thoughts about the absentee parent from the beginning and you'll continue to have them for a long time, but over those twenty one to thirty days you'll notice they become less frequent and your mind will begin to automatically replace the thoughts for you, without having to work at the steps of the process. Some do this with visual aides, like kissing a picture of their child and consciously smiling. Others will verbally say something to themselves that shifts their thinking. Still others use a more tactile approach and pop a rubber band around their wrist to assist in redirecting their thoughts.

Only you know if any of these or a host of other ideas will work for you. Just remember, no one will make a shift of this magnitude seamlessly, and that's ok. You'll continue to think about the other person and have emotions attached to those thoughts. What's important is that you teach yourself how to shift those thoughts to the more productive emotions of love and acceptance. I'm not implying you have to gain acceptance for any wrongs committed against you or your child. The events of the past don't change. What you can change is the way you respond to those negative emotions.

Find acceptance in your situation. Block the negative emotions that only handicap and minimize your ability to function as the caring parent or guardian you are. You'll learn in time to replace those negative emotions with positive regard for your position as the center of your little one's universe.

I'm not asking you to put this book down and work on this process for three weeks or more before reading on. The examples in later chapters help demonstrate why making this shift is so important for your child and yourself. At the same time, I'm also not discouraging the idea either. If you feel it would be better for you to put this book down and focus your energy on this task for the next three weeks, by all means do so.

You can easily pick back up when you've made the shift, although I think the book will only help to motivate and give extra support while making this change. As I said before, only you know the best way to make this shift. It's not important how you get there. It's just important that you do, for your sake and that of your child.

WHAT SHOULD I TELL MY CHILD?

As a young man I was taught an important lesson about answering questions. I've always taken this with me and utilize it, not just in this situation, but in many aspects of my life.

A person asked me to answer only what was asked of me. She then asked, "Do you know what time it is?" I looked at my watch and responded, "It's 11:30". She quickly admonished me saying, "Listen to the question. I didn't ask you what time it is. I asked you if you know what time it is. The answer to that question is 'yes'". She went on to say, "People get themselves in trouble by answering more than is asked of them. They don't think about the actual question. I doubt they even hear the last half of any question". I took that lesson to heart and see it as a cornerstone to this process.

As they get older, your child will ask questions about their absentee parent. As they do, remember this example. Don't just answer a generalization of what you think they might have asked. Take a moment to process their exact wording, and then respond with facts relevant to the exact question asked.

Why do this? Because kids will only ask what they're mentally prepared to receive the answer to. Answering more may be difficult for them to process. In some cases it could be damaging.

I remember sitting on the edge of the tub one evening, watching my son play, when he stunned me with a change of subject. He asked, "Do I have a Mama?" Remembering the example, I took a moment to process what he asked, and then said, "Yes, you do". To which he replied, "Ok".

I ruffled his hair and he went back to playing. I inquired, "Do you have any other questions for me?" He said, "Yes. Why does my rubber duck float wrong?"

He was on to the next subject. He'd asked his question. He was satisfied with the response and consequently he didn't have a need to ask any other questions for several months.

When answering questions about the absentee parent, remember to show them they matter, with love and care. It won't be difficult because you do love them, you do care about them and they do matter to you. If they didn't, you wouldn't have sought the advice in this book. Your child's coming to you in a vulnerable state, which gives you the opportunity to not only answer their question, but also build their self esteem and bring the two of you closer.

This doesn't have to be a horrible discussion. Even though parents raising the children of absentee parents often dread the mention of the other parent, this should be thought of as an opportunity to foster closeness between you and your child and show them how important they are to you. The benefits of approaching these situations in this manner will be felt throughout the course of your child's entire life.

The most difficult part of answering your child's questions also happens to be one of the most important. While you take that moment to determine how to answer their exact question, take a few extra seconds to strip away all emotion and opinion from your answer. Practice your response in your head.

Some parents have a tendency to saddle children with their tainted view of the situation. Make certain not to be one of those parents. Give your child the facts relevant to the question they asked, but don't go so far as to give them you're commentary about the response.

I know there's a strong desire to protect your child, and most parents fear a candy coated response will push their child closer to the absent parent, but I'd caution against relaying your emotional, gut response and here's why.

The absentee parent, regardless of past transgressions, is still your child's biological parent. This puts your child in a strange position. Many feel they have to defend a parent in their absence. The best you can do for your child and your own frustration level is to avoid that situation at all costs. Just give the dry details to the exact question and ask if they have any other questions.

If there are negative aspects to the absentee parent, your child will pick up on them on their own. They don't need anyone else's anger to cloud their objectivity of the situation. They'll come to the conclusions that are appropriate for them. I know most parents fear the child will be hurt further by the absentee parent, which may be a very valid fear, but this is a risk inherent in the circumstances.

At the same time, Don't overly glamorize the situation either. Just give the facts. Giving the child a romanticized or unrealistic view of the situation can be just as harmful as interjecting venom into your responses. Some might think, "This is a difficult tightrope to walk," and they're right. It is, and we're only three chapters into the book. No one said this was an easy topic to tackle but this guide, starting with the understanding that kids only need direct responses to the exact questions they ask, will give you a step by step game plan when the questions do start coming.

Below are both good and bad examples that should give you an idea of the right and wrong way to answer such questions. The following is a potentially harmful response to a question:

Child: Mommy, where is my Daddy?

Mother: Your good for nothing father is living on the beach with that person he left Mommy for.

I can understand how this response might slip out. No one's saying you aren't entitled to a sense of betrayal or emotion over the ending of a relationship or over the absence of another parent but this response is not at all what the child asked. The parent in this example gives their child entirely too much information and includes too many opportunities for the child to defend the parent who isn't there to defend themselves.

This parent is also branding the child with responsibility for the absentee parents' actions by starting the statement with "Your". That word gives the child ownership of someone else's actions and the consequences that follow. Some might go so far as to hear the statement, "Your good for nothing father..." as, "You're good for nothing".

Beyond that, the parent's opening their child to a concept they're not yet mature enough to understand. Children shouldn't be made to grow up too fast and they shouldn't be saddled with the responsibilities of others' decisions.

Let's try another response to the same question:

> Child: Mommy, where is my Daddy?
>
> Mother: Lets see, last I heard he moved to Miami with his friend and they bought a house. I think I heard he was a contractor or something. He....

While she was less emotional, the mother in this example disregarded the first rule of answering her child's question. The child didn't ask anything that would've elicited this kind of response. The child may be too young to be bogged down in the details. Don't make things more complicated than they have to be. The child in this example simply asked where his father is, so they should be given a state or general area. If the answer isn't as specific as the child wants, they'll ask further questions.

Let your child guide you in the amount of information they require at the moment. This is akin to the way a dolphin or a bat would use sonar to hone in on the exact information they're searching for. Keep it simple. Answer exactly what they ask. Remember to tell your child how special they are and how much you love them. You won't go wrong.

Let's try another example:

> Child: Mommy, where is my Daddy?
>
> Mother: He's in Florida, I believe. Do you want to talk about your Daddy?

In this response the mother answers the exact question asked of her. She also ends the statement with, I believe. This leaves open the possibility for changes in information.

It's a good idea not to act certain about things you may not actually know. It's also a good idea to give your child a hug as positive reinforcement when they come to you with questions. They need to know you love them and that they can come to you with any questions they might have. Just by asking, your child is coming to you in a vulnerable state. They're putting a great deal of faith in you and they need your love and reassurance that they're doing the right thing by asking you.

If your child feels they can't come to you – they won't. To some, that may not seem like such a bad thing, but keep this in mind. If your child can't come to you, they'll do one of two things. They'll either get they're information from some other, unfiltered, source or they'll construct they're own responses to whatever questions they may have. Either option is not ideal.

If your child gets their information from someone else, you may have to handle the fallout from a person who didn't have the benefit of reading this book.

As bad as this option may be, a child's invented narratives about their absentee parent will invariably be worse. If a child constructs their own answers to their questions, they'll go to one of two extremes. They'll either paint the absentee parent as a hero, which will automatically make you or themselves the villain – usually both. Or they'll construct such a venomous portrait in their mind they may be prompted to irrational actions. Either one is much more difficult to overcome than following the plan. Answer the exact question asked, when it's asked.

In the event my child asks someone other than me or my wife a question, I have a very firm understanding with family and close friends that they won't give any answers, whatsoever. In my child's case, the family response is, "That's really something you need to ask your Daddy about. He knows more about that than I do". This, of course, is followed by a hug. I've asked that they call and relay, word for word, what was asked so I have time to prepare my answer when he and I are alone. This has happened on occasion. In each case family told me they were glad we practiced exactly what to say. They would've been more likely to respond based on their own feelings without thinking, rather than allowing all information to come from one source.

If you want to give your parents or friends the ability to answer questions your child might pose, for the sake of immediacy, that's definitely your prerogative. There are benefits to handling a question as soon as possible, as you'll read in later chapters. Make certain in those situations each person has read this book or is at least clear about the concepts, before they're alone with your child.

I can imagine a litany of responses given by angered family or impulsive friends. Each could take much more time to triage and deal with, than would be required if you personally handled the response, without assistance. This scenario might even be extended to new spouses or significant others.

When my son, for instance, comes to my wife with questions about the absentee parent, she provides love and reaffirmation, but she also tells him I knew the absentee parent better than anyone else he could ask. She then hugs him and contacts me to either talk to him or to relay exactly what was asked. This is helped a great deal by the fact my wife and I have been trained as therapists. However, I have complete confidence this training is nonessential to develop a patent answer when discussing the absentee parent. This of course assumes your current significant other doesn't personally know the absentee parent and wasn't present before the parent left.

It's also important to note that situations where there is a current significant other, there might be other children involved. It may be a child birth between the single parent and their significant other or children brought into the relationship by the significant other. In these situations it's not only permissible, but advised to be transparent and open with other children involved as well. Anything less opens children to confusion and inappropriate self stories about their past. The last thing any parent wants is for their children to believe they've been lied to, or had something kept from them. We'll discuss this scenario in coming chapters.

Once you've practiced what you're going to say and how you're going to say it... your child will throw you a curve ball. As you know, that's the one thing you can always count on. Your child will surprise you, as we'll discuss further in the next chapter.

WHEN SHOULD I TELL MY CHILD?

I remember asking a large number of people the question, "When do I tell my child about his absentee parent?" I asked ministers and my parents, professors and therapists. I asked other parents in the same position and grandparents who couldn't conceive of the situation, and I received as many responses as the number of people I asked. There was no consensus.

Here's what I myself have discovered. After combing the available research and speaking with everyone who did it wrong, I can tell you exactly when to tell your child about their absentee parent. The perfect time to tell them is… when they're ready. How will you know when that is? When they ask.

That may seem like a ridiculously obvious answer. Admittedly it sounds like something out of a fortune cookie or a piece of cinematic wisdom delivered by a wise old sage (usually bald and blind) to the young hero who isn't ready for the enlightenment.

It sounds that way only until I tell you this. Only one person gave me that answer and she specializes in child psychology and parental alienation. Everyone else gave me a variety of concrete timelines.

Some said wait until they're an adult. Others said tell them everything at once while they're a baby and repeat it until they're old enough to understand. Others gave milestones such as first grade, sixth grade, tenth grade, or the child's senior year. Still others said four, ten, fifteen, eighteen, or twenty one.

I would personally advise against all these options and I say this for several reasons. The first being that a parent who has a distant age in mind isn't taking into account the questions children ask over time. Be receptive to questions as they come. You may not be given a second chance by a child who feels their inquiries fall on deaf ears or are met with hostility.

My second concern; setting your own date to tell the child gives them ample opportunity to make their own determinations about the absentee parent and their role in the situation.

A third thought that comes to mind. The caregiver's timeline may have no regard for the child's developmental level and, as importantly, their desired level of disclosure. The child may not be to a point mentally or emotionally to appropriately process the information the parent wants to give. The parent's information may also be more than they would ever choose to know. As said before, you may have a child who either can't, or chooses not to, handle the baggage they're handed.

Fourth and finally, even a child who's ready, willing, and waiting to hear about their absentee parent will likely have difficulty receiving the entire story in one sitting. That's not to say you won't have a "dam-break" moment, when your child asks a flood of questions. You will, but remember, they need to be in control of the flow of information through their questions, not your pre conceived notion of a quintessential "right time".

Here are a couple of examples to consider. The first are examples of what not to do when it comes to talking to your child about an absentee parent. Consider in the first illustration that the father has just gotten off the phone, after an argument with the absentee parent.

Father: Honey, could you come in here?

Daughter: Yes Daddy?

Father: You were asking questions about your
            Mother? I have some things to tell you.

There are several issues in this example. First and foremost, the child didn't ask anything. Her father volunteered information, and in doing so, the child's not in the proper mindset to receive whatever information he has for her. Her mind knows what it can handle and will only allow her to ask the information it's prepared to receive.

Second, the father has just been in an argument with the absentee parent, so he's much more likely to speak from a place of emotion, rather than speaking to the child using passion free facts.

There are times to be passionate. Be passionate about how happy you are that your child came to you. Be passionate about your adoration for your child. Answering absentee parent questions is not the time to have emotion. Your child will pick up on the stress and may be less likely to feel they can come to you, or worse. They may feel they're to blame for the situation.

Third, the father seems to be preparing to tell his daughter something negative about her mother. Although it can be difficult at times, refrain from doing so at all costs. If your child asks specific questions that elicit answers about the absentee parents negative qualities, so be it. (E.g. Did Daddy snore? Do you know if Mama ever spent time in prison?) Those, of course are light hearted examples.

But in all seriousness, avoid the negative when it comes to the absentee parent. If there are negative traits to be seen in the absentee parent, a child won't need any help uncovering them. There's nothing positive to be gained by letting children in on their absentee parent's negative qualities without specific requests that happen to illicit such responses. In fact, as noted before, doing so could easily put a child in a position where they feel they need to defend their absentee parent.

In this second example, consider that the parent has had a stressful day at work. She picked her son up from school and is in the middle of a grocery store trying to finish shopping, before picking up a younger son at daycare.

Son: Mommy, does Daddy hate me?

Mother: Why do you ask these questions? You always ask at the worst times. Ask Mommy after dinner.

Instead of reprimanding the child in this example, the mother could've handled the situation differently. It's easy to snap, especially depending on the situation. It's important however to hold your temper and try not to make the mistake this mother did. Avoid at all costs, getting upset with your child for asking a question about their absentee parent. Your child's coming to you in a vulnerable state. They need support and love and you'll provide it as you have throughout their little lives.

Telling the child in this example to ask later, at an opportune time, is not the best way to handle the situation. This child would be unlikely to broach the subject after dinner. In fact, it's more likely this child would never turn to the parent again. It's important to understand how difficult this situation would be for the child in this example. The emotion you, as a parent, feel being asked about an absentee parent can be anxiety producing, even crushing. Imagine how much more stress a child has to feel, preparing to ask these same questions.

Let's look at a different way this situation could've been handled. Imagine instead the mother stops whatever she's doing, moves to the side of the store aisle and responds in a manner closer to this:

Son: Mommy, why does Daddy hate me?

Mother: Your Daddy doesn't hate you. Come give Mommy a hug. Nobody hates you. You're my special little man. Would you like to talk about him?

In this example, the mother attends to the exact question asked. She shows affection. She reaffirms the child and tells him how much he means to her. She then opens the door for her child to ask further questions if needed. In this way she attends to his needs while building self esteem, and all in a matter of seconds. This mother answers the question, then shows her child the love he deserves, just as you do.

That being said, listen for questions. If you answer – they will come. Pay attention for small questions and reassure your child, it's ok for them to ask. In doing so you not only ensure they'll come to you with other questions about their absentee parent. You also greatly increase the chances they'll come with other, just as important, issues. In the process, you'll build a relationship that contributes to your child's safety. Not to mention the added bonus that you'll be more involved in their life as they grow. Most children start with simple questions like, "Do I have a daddy?", or "Why don't I have a mommy?" These progress to questions like, "Can I read the court paperwork or your documentation for myself?" or "Tell me exactly what happened when they left us".

While the following instance doesn't specifically point to an issue dealing with absentee parents, my child provided an illustration of children asking what they want, when they want, without regard for their surroundings. These are not situations children should be reprimanded for because, especially in my child's case, inferences were made based on information I, the parent, had given him.

We were in a crowded grocery store on New Years Eve buying the necessary accoutrements to make hot dogs. He leaned towards me in the seat of the basket and whispered, "Daddy is it ok to count?" I'll consider those famous last words from now on. I quickly responded, "Sure thing, Boogie Bear" (One of many nicknames).

My son leaned towards the shopping cart next to us and started counting, "1, 2, 3, up to 9, 9 wine bottles. Look Daddy, that lady has 9 bottles of wine. Look at her. She must be an alcoholic. Daddy, we shouldn't be like her".

I dropped the ball. I was so taken off guard by the statement, I turned to the woman and said, "Umm. Wow. Hmm". I quickly walked down the pet food aisle. For the record, the only pet we had at the time was a male Beta fish named Dorothy and Dorothy needed no food. My first response was to remove my child and myself from the line of fire of the potentially bottle wielding woman with the arsenal of $4 grocery store wine.

Of course, I didn't think we'd be hit with a barrage of long necks. She seemed like a very nice, understanding woman who was more than likely assigned the task of getting materials for the zero hour toast later that night. She didn't deserve that sort of labeling, and I know I never told my little one that everyone who drinks is an alcoholic. I have however, talked to him on many occasions about the dangers of alcohol, smoking, and any of a number of other common and generally accepted vices. So how did he materialize that; by calling out that poor woman in a grocery store on New Years Eve.

This just serves to illustrate the point, kid's questions and statements can and will come at the most inopportune moments and in the most inappropriate places. Be as prepared as a person can be for the unusual and inconvenient questions. They no doubt will happen.

No matter how simple or tough the question, parents always feel pressure. They always feel unprepared to answer, be it a question about absentee parents or a statement about the lush in the next checkout lane.

That's where this book comes in. Everyone is thrown on occasion, but by reading this book, you mentally and emotionally prepare yourself better than the vast majority of parents and guardians who find themselves in the position of fielding questions about an absentee parent.

Some children don't come right out and ask questions. This provides an extra level of stress, confusion and challenge for parents, if they don't know what to look for. By noticing the signs, you place yourself in a position that better prepares you for the difficult questions, when and as they come.

In my child's case, my wife and I have noticed he only rarely comes out and asks a question without taking several days to contemplate. He's mentioned before that he's afraid he'll hurt his Mom's (my wife's) feelings or my own by asking about the absentee parent. This gave us the opportunity, as a couple, to reassure him we wouldn't be hurt by any question he asks and that we're happy to answer whatever questions he might have.

Rather than feeling aggravation and stress every time a child comes to their parent with questions. They should instead think of it as an occasion to tell their child they're loved and bring the relationship closer. The child is presenting their parent with an amazing opportunity and they'll do a great job when they take it.

I suspect my son is also trying to decide mentally and emotionally whether he wants to hear the answer to the question he's considering. In his case, the four to six days prior to asking a big question is filled with appetite and behavior changes, multiple subtle hints about the question he's preparing to ask, and a search for correlations in his life that give a hint to the question he's about to hit Daddy with.

By noticing this trend, I allow myself half a week to prepare for the question he's about to ask. I doubt his subconscious motivation is to make certain Daddy's not blindsided. It's possible he's taking time to practice the question in his mind before he asks.

Twice I've noticed the trend extend longer than a week, in these cases I sat down with my son and asked if he had anything to ask. On one occasion he did. The other time he said he didn't have any questions and asked if he could go play. He returned to his normal routine quickly. In the latter case, I believe he decided he didn't want the answer to the question on his mind and chose instead to go back to life as usual. This may have been a protective measure for a young mind unprepared to process the information, whatever it may be.

A point worth remembering in this example is that I opened the door and gave him a forum, in case he wanted to ask a question, and I only did so at obvious signs he was planning to ask a question. It's important not to force a child to ask a question they aren't ready to ask, just like its important a parent not give them information laced with baggage or information they haven't asked for.

In my son's case, he wasn't mentally or emotionally in a place where he felt secure in asking his question. I respected that and didn't push him. Forcing the issue of an absentee parent has as much negative emotion and apprehension attached for the child as it does for the parent or guardian. As said before, there's usually more anxiety and fear for the child than the parent. It's beneficial to recognize and acknowledge how difficult it must be for your child to ask their questions.

Tell them you understand it might not be easy for them to come to you with questions. Reassure them they're doing the right thing. Remind them how much you love them, while answering the exact question they ask, nothing more.

Unfortunately children rarely find an opportune moment to ask their difficult questions, but it's important to answer whenever they come. Set aside whatever you're doing. Sit with them and attend to their needs.

Some ask, "What if my child's too young?" The answer to that question is - they won't be. Children mature at different rates. One of the wonders of the human mind is that it'll rarely allow you to ask a question if you aren't mentally prepared to receive the answer.

A spouse asking if their significant other is cheating may be devastated by the response, but their mind has already worked through the eventuality and probability the answer is yes before they ask. A child's mind works in much the same way. A child can come up with far worse scenarios in their mind than a parent can deliver, so it's best not to delay answers.

Of course, a grave error usually occurs when someone answers more than their child asks. They're prepared for their question; not always for the parents expanded answer.

Along the same vein, others ask, "When should I tell them everything?" You know the answer at this point. It won't all come at once. Let them determine when they get information and how much they receive. Just be there to answer the questions when, and as they come. You'll have a series of discussions with your child over the years, in which all the information will be discussed. Thankfully, it's exceedingly rare for a child to request a large amount of information early on. In the vast majority of cases they instead ask the same questions repeatedly, over time, and accept the small bites of information as they receive them.

The only caveat I can share from my own experiences is that my child once overheard a relative mention that a book of custody documentation exists. He asked, as a five year old, to have the book read to him. I believe he assumed it to be like the Dr. Seuss and Golden books we read to him nightly.

I told him I was proud of him for coming to me. I was happy to talk to him about it. The book was his and he was welcome to read it when he was older, but I wanted him to be old enough to read and understand the words. I told him I wanted him to ask again in the future, when he felt he was ready to read the whole book.

I have no doubt that day will come and when it does, he'll receive the book and have free and open access to the whole body of information – the good, the bad and the ugly. If there's a lesson to this story it's that little ears never stop listening. Try to avoid discussing anything with an adult; you aren't prepared to answer for and never assume anything's over their head. An off hand comment or a moment of vocal frustration can quickly translate into an innocent question with a very adult answer.

It's akin to the child who doesn't blindly accept that babies just come from tummies and get there through love. Or the child who presses about the logistics of Santa visiting every single home in the world in one night. In these cases, use your judgment. Determine what prompted the adult question. If it's due to a tip off they've received, an altered response may be advisable.

HOW SHOULD I TELL MY CHILD?

By this point you've already read chapters filled with information on how to tell your child about an absentee parent. But it's a subject worthy of its own chapter. I've had to search my memory to find examples of my child asking questions about his absentee parent, because in all honesty he hasn't asked that many questions compared to the multitude of questions about robots, stars, and bodily functions. He can go six months to a year without asking a single absentee parent question. At the same time, the number of questions has increased recently to one every couple of months. I suspect most children progress in this same fashion.

Some ask, "How do I even tell them? Their father was so mean and abusive" or, "I was so hurt by her mother's departure. How do I follow your guide and not include all that pain and fear and rejection?" It's simple. You just don't. It's important to remember the negative emotions are yours. They don't have to be your child's. In fact, the hurt and pain won't affect your child, to the same magnitude, unless you allow it to.

I've heard people rightfully say, "The absentee parent's such a bad influence or such a damaged person. I can't in good conscience tell them otherwise". I'm not asking anyone to sugar coat the absentee parent's story or push their child into a relationship with a dangerous person. Doing so would be irresponsible and damaging to the child.

That being said, a parent owes it to their child to answer only the exact question their child asks, free from emotion, stating only the relevant facts. Facts about the absentee parent are not nearly as important as the relationship between parent and child.

Let them bring up the subject. Show them love and consideration and model for them what a positive parental relationship should be. A person told me they informed their four year old that Daddy was in prison for killing someone. I asked if their child had actually asked, "Is my Daddy in prison?" She replied, "No, but I wanted her to know what kind of man he is".

These decisions don't help the child. They can only hurt. Your child will ask these questions eventually, but there's no reason to force information they may not be equipped to handle. A child with too much information will be likely to make determinations about themselves, based on the information in front of them. It'd be easy for a child to tell themselves, "Daddy is a bad person and he's my Daddy, so I must be a bad person". Of course, nothing could be further from the truth, but you don't want to be the parent having to combat thoughts like these. One idea of this nature can set off a chain of events that are exceedingly difficult to recover from.

I remember my son asking whether or not he would leave his kids when he grew up. That gave me an opportunity to instill in him that parents don't leave their children. I didn't leave him, my wife wouldn't leave and he wouldn't leave his own children because kids are the most important thing in the world to parents.

Children obviously understand that the absentee parent left at some point. When the opportunity presents itself there's no harm in reminding them that you haven't and you won't. Children appreciate affirmation. They know in their heart you aren't going anywhere, but it's always nice to hear it from the parent's mouth. Never take for granted the impact your reassurances have on your child.

Any time a child comes to you with information of this nature, they're doing so in part to gauge your response. You have an opportunity in that moment to either validate their worst thoughts about themselves, or to correct these thoughts and replace them with warm, positive feelings and thoughts that'll put them back on the track you, as a parent, want them on.

This course correction of sorts could potentially change the trajectory of their entire lives. When in doubt, hug them; tell them you love them and that you're proud of them. This is a good rule of thumb in general, regardless of the situation or question.

With this knowledge, it's a good idea to practice how you plan to talk to your child. Don't wing it. You may not know exactly what your child will ask, but you can prepare for the way you respond. You can practice in your mind, in the car at a light, on the treadmill at the gym or during a commercial break after they go to bed. Where ever you do it – do it.

Be prepared, children love the unexpected. They'll invariably hit you with something you don't see coming. As said before, the way you respond to these inquiries is just as important as what you say. Practice smiling and think about hugging them. Imagine telling them you love them while you answer.

Whatever the content of your discussion, it's imperative not to act upset or surprised. Your response could affect whether they come to you with future questions. It could even set the tone for your relationship for years to come. Foster an open atmosphere where they know they can come to you with any questions or concerns. Whatever the question and whatever the facts, you have to tell them. Just remember: Be frank. Be honest. Be supportive. Be kind. If you can follow this mantra everything else is just details.

WHERE SHOULD I TELL MY CHILD?

I remember watching my son play on a fast food playground before my wife and I married. He performed his occasional fly by pattern to hydrate. He seemed to think a child in motion couldn't be asked to leave. I used my time during these play sessions to study and read while watching him ensure a good nights sleep.

One evening fly by held a different trajectory than patterns past. He jumped in my lap and asked, "Is it my fault my Mama left me?"

I have to admit, he brought a lump to my throat. I held him close and hugged him. I said, "No son, it's not your fault. Don't ever think it's your fault".

I hugged him again and told him I loved him. I asked if he had any other questions and he replied, "No".

I asked, "Was there anything that made you feel that way?"

He responded, "Yeah, that girl asked where my Mama was and I told her I didn't have one. She asked if it was my fault my Mom left. I told her I'd come ask....so I did".

I told him what a special boy he was and told him he could go tell her it wasn't his fault. He hugged me, and then took off to play again. Questions can come anytime, anywhere and you have to prepare yourself to answer, wherever you receive them.

In an ideal world your child would wait until you're spending quiet time alone with them at the end of the evening to spring the difficult questions on you. Unfortunately for us, most kids, including my own, aren't wired that way. My son's questions have tended to come while Daddy's studying for a big test or walking out the door to head to class.

Your child will no doubt ask their most important questions in the middle of a crowded department store, or at an incredibly important moment, when your mind is focused on something else – say avoiding a crash up ahead in traffic. There you are, skidding sideways, trying to save everyone in the car from utter annihilation, when a question comes from the back seat, "Why did my parent leave?" On paper it may seem slightly amusing, especially to those who have experienced this already, but at that moment… it's not.

Children can't help it. It's not something they plan. They feel a stressful situation coming, and they revert back to the most stressful question on their mind. This may be akin to pulling the band aid off quickly. It'll still hurt but since you're hurting anyway, now's as good a time as any.

When these situations present themselves it's easy to answer in the wrong way, or with the wrong information. That's why you're here – to avoid that, and that's what you have to do, avoid the wrong message or delivery at all costs. If possible, move them to a quiet place with the least distractions possible to answer the question. If you don't have that option, answer the question wherever you are. In the case of the impending accident, find a reasonable exit and ask them to repeat the question.

Some children may find comfort in asking their questions in loud, distracting places, as I suspect mine does. This makes it more difficult to focus solely on them, and allows them the chance to distract themselves if they don't like the response. In this way, potential bad news is delivered as a glancing blow.

This is extended to the child who asks questions in front of siblings who may not share the same history. In these situations it's advisable to avoid a scenario whereby you chance alienating the sibling by asking them to leave the room or otherwise remove themselves from the immediate vicinity. While they might not share the same history, the situation is a part of their history as well. As mentioned before, not allowing the sibling to hear information about the absentee parent causes the information to become a secret or something that should be hidden.

This behavior can also make all children involved feel there's a reason to be ashamed. Or that your family situation is not up to the standard of others. This can only hurt the family and is, of course, far from the truth.

While I wouldn't seek the sibling out and force them to hear answers they might not have any interest in, I'd also speak freely in front of them about the situation, if asked. Be open and frank, no matter what immediate family members are around. Take the time in advance to ensure siblings and other family members do not contradict, or add to your responses or add their own inquiries to the child's question. Few scenarios can derail this plan faster than an angry relative who refuses to take part in this method. I've mentioned before but it bears repeating, it's always a good idea make certain everyone is on the same page where your discussion plan is concerned.

It's also common for the child who doesn't have an absentee parent, to come to you with questions about the absentee parent. The handling of this situation is very much determined by the sibling's maturity and reasons for asking. If it's for means of hurting their sibling, I'd avoid answering questions; otherwise feel free to answer – to a point. I'd never allow a sibling to have more information about the absentee parent or the situation than the involved child. This is done for understandable reasons. By nature, children will say things at inopportune times. There's no reason to give the sibling added ammunition that might be innocently told at an inappropriate or harmful time.

In cases where your child comes to you with a question about their absentee parent, sit down wherever reasonable, so you can place them on your knee or hold them while talking. Eye contact is essential, and above all else be nice. Answer exactly what they ask. Show them you love them and are happy they're comfortable enough to ask the question. No matter the situation, try not to appear rattled, however jarring the question may be.

Your composure won't only make the situation go more smoothly, it'll do two other important things we discussed earlier: Open the channels of communication, making your future relationship more stable, and model to them how to behave as an adult and parent.

Humans tend to revert, in stressful situations, to the behaviors they were taught as children. This can be reduced with planning and awareness of which modeled behaviors from your childhood you approve of, because you'll invariably, without work on your part, end up sounding or acting like your parents.

In this same way your level of composure will be matched by your child in later years under stressful circumstances. This may be for better or worse. In your case, I prefer to believe for the better.

THE PROCESS

This chapter serves more as a review of the process than an introduction of new material. I want to provide a clear, concise appraisal for you to examine before we discuss the pitfalls every caregiver should be aware of when discussing the absentee parent with their child. You can also utilize this chapter as a quick review of essential material in coming years.

Whenever your child comes to you with a question about their absentee parent, what do you do? What do you say? What's running through your mind? The reading thus far should've given a good foundation for those questions.

When your child comes to you with a question of this nature, put down whatever you're doing (safety permitting) and shift your focus to your child and their question. Pay special attention to the question itself. Think about the exact wording your child used when asking the question. Don't be afraid to ask your child to repeat what they've asked. When they do so, clear your mind and hang on their every word. It's better to have your child repeat their question, than to answer a general idea of what you thought you heard.

This is a difficult but worthy trait for the vast majority of parents to master. The mere mention of an absentee parents name can elicit immediate thoughts, emotions and fears internally. It would be easy for instinct and shear adrenalin to overwhelm a caregiver faced with their child's latest question. As difficult as it may be, parents should find a way to quail this surge of neural connections and chemical responses in their own mind.

When your child asks a question, devote your attention to your little one and when possible, get down on their level, physically. You might kneel on one knee or sit them in your lap when you talk to them. It's always a good idea to look them in the eye and smile while you take the two moments we've discussed in previous chapters.

In the first of those two moments, analyze the exact words your child used when asking their question and craft an answer that only addresses the specifics of their inquiry. Utilize the second moment to strip all emotion from the answer you're preparing to give your child. Go through the exercise of seeing how much emotion you can take from your answer, mentally. Then go back and remove the rest. Ask a trusted friend or family member to help you practice, if needed.

After crafting your response, it comes time to focus on the delivery of your answer. Look your child in the eye and give the emotion free response that covers only the exact question asked.

Please be aware though, while the response itself should be free from emotion, you cannot be. A child receiving a response from an unemotional caregiver might feel their guardian doesn't care about the situation and by extension, them.

Show your child you care as deeply for them as you and I know you do. Give them a hug and a smile before answering the question. Tell them how proud you are they came to you. If need be, repeat the question to ensure you accurately assessed the information they're hoping to receive. Then answer the question they've asked – nothing more, nothing less. If there's a question of how much to give, err on the side of less information rather than more. If need be, they'll ask further questions.

Once you've answered the question, remind your child how much you love them. Ask them if they have any other questions and reiterate how proud you are they came to you.

If they do have other questions, follow the same pattern. A common parenting mistake is to follow this guide for the first two questions, then get comfortable and try to wing it for the third question and beyond. You'll find this won't work as well as following the plan. There're several hazards you avoid by following this process, all of which will be discussed in the following chapters.

THE PITFALLS

This portion of the book is every bit as important as the first half. Why is that? These seven pitfalls aren't mistakes a few people have made. These are made by the vast majority of parents. In fact, any given single parent, guardian, or parent with a significant other is likely to commit at least two of these pitfalls at some point while telling their child about an absentee parent.

What does that do? If a parent commits any one of these pitfalls, let alone multiple infractions, it could be detrimental to their child's emotional and relational development and their ability to cope with this delicate situation. The parent may not see the back lash immediately, but rest assured any one of these pitfalls will harm communication between them and their child at some

71

point in the future. It could make a situation involving the absentee parent more difficult than it has to be.

How do you avoid these common mistakes? The first thing you can do is be aware of what the pitfalls are. Then examine and know yourself well enough to know which ones you're most likely to make. Once you've done those two things, you can begin to craft your responses around fact-based objectivity that minimizes the occurrence of any one of these pitfalls.

Some pitfalls have been mentioned in prior chapters. This was done as a matter of presenting the most relevant, useful examples. This doesn't detract from the importance of the information. If anything it should help to emphasize how necessary it is to avoid these pitfalls.

In future chapters I'll discuss each of the pitfalls in greater depth. However in this chapter I've chosen to simply list them. This is done to provide you with a concise list to look over when reviewing the important points of this book in the future, which I wholeheartedly recommend. I'd advice against spending all your time ruminating on any one subject, but a proper amount of planning prior to the event will provide a higher likelihood for positive results.

That being said, the seven pitfalls all parents and guardians should avoid when telling a child about their absentee parent are:

1. Blaming the child

2. Forcing the issue

3. Answering more than they ask

4. Telling before they're ready

5. Being overly critical

6. Sugar coating or creating martyrs

7. Lying

The chapters that follow give a better understanding of each pitfall and why each is damaging to your child. The chapters also provide tips to help you avoid the mistakes most parents make. In the process, you should be able to strengthen your communication and relationship with your child.

BLAMING THE CHILD

This is one of the most common and emotional pitfalls caregivers are unintentionally guilty of. As discussed repeatedly in earlier chapters, the topic of absentee parents is often charged with deep, instant emotion. Be it a single mother whose husband is no longer around, a single father whose girlfriend left behind a child, or grandparents and friends who don't know the location of either parent. In any case, there tends to be a very real and understandable feeling of betrayal, disappointment or abandonment. If not these, a host of other possible negative emotions are evoked whenever the topic's raised.

It's important to remember children don't ask about their absentee parent out of any sense of hostility or disregard for their parents feelings. Children have their own feelings and personal stories they're trying to work through, and doing so requires two things only a parent or guardian can provide: your support and an answer to their questions.

The answer can be "I don't know", if you truly don't. I'd suggest only using that answer if it's actually the case. Children are walking polygraphs, or lie detectors. They'll know if they're being lied to. It's not worth taking the risk.

A large percentage of caregivers see a child's questions about their absentee parent as a personal affront or suggestion that they aren't doing an adequate job. If you find you have this response to questions about the absentee parent, please put those thoughts out of your head.

A caregiver can easily wonder why their child is asking about an absentee parent. Put yourself in their little shoes. They're curious. This is the same child that asked some question like, "Why am I able to put my foot in mouth?" just before showing you they could. Kids want to know everything about their surroundings. That includes close relationships or a conspicuous lack thereof.

Here are a few examples I've heard, of parents answering similar questions about absentee parents. There are both less and more appropriate responses:

Child: Daddy, why don't I have a mommy? Other kids do.

Dad: Am I not doing a good enough job? Is there
         something the other kids' moms are doing, I'm
         not?

This father set in motion the possibility his child will never speak to him about anything important, ever again. It can be difficult at times to control emotions when discussing the absentee parent. However, it's imperative not to answer a child in a hostile manner, whatever they ask. As said before, when kids ask questions about their absentee parent don't take it personally. The example above may seem extreme, but I've heard countless stories of parent responses that were every bit as harsh or worse.

Parents who answer in this fashion are understandably upset about the other parent's lack of involvement in their child's life. The parent no doubt harbors emotions about the way they and the child were treated. It's a difficult balancing act, playing mother and father. In cases where parents respond in this manner, they recount a sense they were doing a substandard job. They felt their child was implying the absentee parent would fill a void left by the single parent's inadequacies.

I've also heard a similar version of events from formerly single parents who've remarried or in some other way brought a significant other into the child's life. In these cases the parent or person filling the parental void feel such questions point out something they, as new parents, are doing wrong. Of course this is not what the child intends when asking about their absentee parent.

When in doubt, assume positive intent. Believe your child's asking any question for the most positive and benign reason possible, because that's the case in the vast majority of children. They don't want to hurt their parent. They just want to know who they are.

When you receive one of these questions from your child, take your moment to focus on what your child's asking. Take your second moment to smile lovingly while striping all emotion from your answer. Then give them what they need.

A more appropriate response might be:

> Child: Daddy, why don't I have a mommy? Other kids do.

> Dad: I'm glad you asked. You do have a mother. She doesn't live with us. (Hugging his child) I love you and I'm proud of you for coming to me. Do you have any other questions?

In this example, the father fields the same question in a more appropriate way. He gets down on the child's level and gives them affirmation for coming to him. He then answers the question, "Why don't I have a mommy?" Once this is done, he follows up by reiterating how much he loves his child and how proud he is. He then opens the possibility for his child to ask further questions, if needed.

Usually this last tactic will only result in one or two more questions, if any. However, allowing your child the opportunity to continue talking about a difficult subject will open the lines of communication for the future and foster a feeling in your child they can come to you with other, equally important, questions and concerns, on a number of subjects.

In my own experience, I'll admit the two moment rule has been an immense help when answering questions for my son. In the beginning, seemingly benign questions would elicit an emotional response from me as well. I remember being single, cooking my son dinner, while paying attention to the Nick Jr. program he was watching. I was thinking about what needed to be done before his bath, when he asked, "Aren't mommy's supposed to cook dinners for kids?"

My gut reaction as I smiled at him was, is he serious? I'm the only person, besides his grandparents, who knows what he likes. What's wrong with the dinner I'm cooking?

After that split second, I thought to myself, what exactly did he ask? He asked, "Aren't mommy's supposed to cook dinners for kids?"

I took my moment to rid myself of the fleeting thoughts. I knew in my heart he wasn't asking out of malice, or to undermine the job I was doing. I turned away from the stove, got down on his level, hugged him, and responded, "Mommy's can make dinners and so can daddies. Why do you ask?"

He fired back, "I'm watching Little Bill and his Mommy just made him dinner". To which I responded, "You know something, you're right, Little Bill's Mom did make him dinner. That's really smart of you to notice. Have you ever seen Little Bill's Dad make him dinner?"

He thought for a second and replied, "Nope, I saw him make breakfast, but I'll bet he's no good at dinner". I laughed and gave him another hug. I said, "You may be right. Do you have any other questions, little man?" He asked, "Can we have what Little Bill's having for dinner?" I responded, "I've got dinner going for tonight. Remind me and you can help me make it tomorrow night". He went about the business of Little Bill and his cartoon eating habits.

Keep in mind when telling a child about their absentee parent, a child's situation is not their fault. It may not be the parents fault either, but children have no more control over their situation than they have over the color of their hair or eyes. It's equally important to remind them as well, that parenting situations are beyond their control and blame. With this in mind, choosing the pitfall of blaming a child for wanting to know about their absentee parent sets the child on a path that pushes them away from their parent and closer to the absentee parent.

If this pitfall feels like it might be possible to commit, guard against it at all costs. If you see you've answered questions in this manner, there's still hope. When you approach your child's questions, on any subject, in the manner you've learn in this book, you begin to mend any bridges that may need repair.

So take your time. Answer their questions and understand that your little one doesn't want to hurt you. They just want to know about themselves and their past. No one can be blamed for that.

FORCING THE ISSUE

Another common pitfall occurs when parents force their child to talk about their absentee parent. Avoid the impulse to commit this pitfall as well. As said in earlier chapters, children only ask the specific questions they're prepared to handle. Questions will come few and far between in early childhood, accelerating as they get older. Some parents feel a need to force answers to questions they haven't been asked. Avoid the urge. Give your child the time they need to mentally prepare for each answer.

This is akin to hatching a butterfly's cocoon on your own schedule. It takes as long as it takes. No amount of hurrying can accelerate the plan. You can watch and get impatient, but nothing will speed the transformation. Whether a hatching butterfly or an inquisitive child, it's best to sit back and enjoy the time you have. Try not to worry about the next step. Any attempt to actively speed the process could harm the little insect, or in our case the child, which serves no productive purpose.

I originally gave the example of a person trying to speed the preparation of a turkey dinner. I remember the disastrous results I endured as a bachelor when I attempted to speed the process of cooking a turkey in my oven. If it took four hours on 400, I was sure the bird only needed to cook two and a half hours on broil. A note to myself and readers: Directions exist for a reason – follow them. Otherwise you end up with a loft apartment full of smoke, a blaring smoke alarm that calls the fire department, and a charred carcass that would make Mr. Kingsford himself proud.

It later dawned on me that, while I had this experience, others might say you can always deep fry the bird. That may be so, but there's no method that makes forcing the issue of an absentee parent acceptable. For this reason, the cocoon analogy makes more sense.

All too often, parents tell me their child's behind the curve. They don't feel their child knows as much as they should about their absentee parent, so they decide to catch their child up. My first response to these parents is always, "Where is this curve and why didn't I know about it?" Just for the record, there is no curve and if there was, your child and mine wouldn't fit into it. Each child is right where they're supposed to be on the so-called curve. A child won't get ahead of their place on the curve, and they won't lag behind. Their mind won't let them. If they haven't asked a question yet, there's a reason. Allow them to be where they are on the continuum.

I'll admit it's tempting to follow your own schedule. Again avoid the urge. All too often a parent, including myself, thinks, I guess it's time for my child to hear more.

Don't do it. If they didn't ask, they don't want to know. It may be painful sometimes, but this whole process is about the child – not the parent. As said before, shift the focus to them.

It's been discussed earlier, but a hidden facet to this pitfall is other people. Sometimes relatives and friends have their own schedules in mind. This can be dangerous when they decide you aren't telling your child as much as they would, or as quickly.

In these situations it's entirely possible a family member, friend, or significant other will give information before the child's ready. For this reason, it's imperative to have a conversation with anyone who might have these conversations with your child. Remind them it's your responsibility alone to relay information about the absentee parent. Walk through the process with them and try to secure confirmations from each person that they'll defer all absentee parent questions to you as the parent or guardian.

It's for this reason siblings should never have more information about a child's absentee parent than the child has. This kind of information has a tendency to find its way back to the child at inopportune times. The child can rightfully see it as a betrayal that people who aren't directly involved have more information than they do.

If you have multiple children in this situation, have a discussion with your older children about directing younger children to you instead of answering questions, unless they're also mature enough to go through this process and understand the importance of not forcing the issue or telling their sibling too much, too soon.

You'll have plenty of opportunities to field questions as your child grows. Don't rush. Your child will want to know everything, probably before you want them to. Let the questions take their own course.

As your child grows older and starts asking the harder questions, you'll ask yourself, "Why are they forcing it?" A small child with forced information about their absentee parent is likely to think the exact same thing, "Why are they telling me things I don't want to know yet?"

It's a difficult pitfall to avoid, but by remembering you'll have ample opportunity to answer your child's questions, the desire to force the issue can be subdued. Let them direct the conversation. You'll both have an easier time with the experience and will enjoy the closeness you gain.

ANSWERING MORE THAN THEY ASK

This pitfall is rooted in a lesson discussed earlier in the book that most don't follow: only answer the question asked of you when discussing absentee parents. This is one pitfall most are guilty of.

Answering more than a child asks is quite different from the pitfall discussed in the last chapter. Forcing the issue involves following an arbitrary schedule the parent conjures in their mind. Where as, the pitfall of answering too much is triggered specifically by the parent who neglects to hear their child's entire question, before answering as they choose. Forcing the issue is initiated by the parent, while answering too much is instigated when a child asks a question.

Some might ask which pitfall is more detrimental to a child. The short answer? Each pitfall has a negative effect and varying degrees of harm are difficult to judge. With this in mind, the pitfall of answering more than they ask is well worth further discussion.

On one level the temptation to release more information to a child than they ask can be almost irresistible. On another, most are guilty of this pitfall out of a sheer lack of attention. This isn't meant as an insult. The vast majority of parents, myself included, are guilty of catching just the gist of a child's statement on any and every subject, feeling they know exactly what their child asked.

I had no idea how much information I was missing during everyday conversations, until I took a doctoral psychology course in active listening. I had the general gist of conversations but was missing enough information I should probably officially apologize to anyone I ever spoke with prior to the fall of 2005.

In most cases, it seems enough to get a general idea of what a child's saying. If a parent hears their child say, "Show and tell is tomorrow", and if they know the letter of the week is "R", that's usually enough to make sure they have a toy robot or stuffed raccoon in their backpack before the next morning.

On occasion however, by catching the high points, a parent picks up on the show and tell portion of the conversation, but somehow misses that they've been volunteered to supply the class with red icing cupcakes and rubber bands. I think most of us have been there at one point or another. Whether parents finds themselves asking, "What do you mean it's picture day?", or "She said I told her it was ok to bring a 'what' to school?" You can see how just "catching the gist" isn't always enough.

That being said, it's also possible for a parent to think they know what's coming only to move in a direction contrary to their child's actual question.

This applies to questions about the absentee parent as well. It's a regular happening. A child simply asks, "Do I have a daddy?" That question requires a simple, "Yes, you do", or "No, you don't", answer.

Parents tend to get a charge of adrenalin when their child asks a question about the absentee parent. Feelings start to well up inside and before the moment passes, the child's question has. It's ok to ask a child to repeat their question. It helps a child feel their parent is invested in the conversation and ensures they'll get a serious answer, instead of a glossy, unrelated response.

Unfortunately a sizable percentage of parents, instead, answer what they think their child asked or what they intuitively feel is the next logical chunk of information, instead of listening to their little one's actual wording. If the parent answers exactly what their child asked, they'll ask follow up questions, if the child decides they want more information. That is, of course, as long as they feel safe in doing so.

Here's an actual example I overheard four years ago. I was taken by the conversation because my son was too young to ask questions at that point. It was the first time I was hit with the realization; I would be in the same spot someday. In the middle of a movie theater line, this child asked, "Mommy, what's my Daddy's name?"

I remember the mother started by saying, "Well he doesn't live with us. I don't know why. He had other things he had to do. That's just the type of person he is. He left me too…"

This mother poured her heart out for what felt like an eternity. When she finished, she mustered a smile. She looked at the child, who stared back blankly. After a long pause, he looked as though she hadn't spoken and asked, "What's his name?"

At that moment I thought the child wasn't even paying attention. I thought about how frustrating the conversation must be for the parent. I hoped my child wouldn't respond in that fashion… when he did eventually speak.

It wasn't until over a year later, after in depth research, that my view of that day's interaction completely changed. I realized it must have been the child who was frustrated.

He asked a simple question but his mother poured her heart out for three minutes about how she was wronged by the father as much, if not more, than the child. She didn't answer his question at all. He only asked his fathers name. A simple Carlos, Jayden or Jacob was all he needed. Anything more was not only unsolicited, it seemed unwanted.

As said before, there's a reason children ask questions in this manner. Their mind carefully selects verbiage based on the amount of information it feels it can handle. In some ways it's a protective factor. A child's mind guards against asking more than they can emotionally handle. This is a theme repeated throughout the book – a child will only ask what they're prepared to grasp.

Of course their careful mental planning does no good, if their parent answers without enough information to know exactly what's being asked. In this way, a child can be harmed by a response, if the answer's not measured, well thought out, and delivered in direct response to their question.

Some parents read this and say things like, "You aren't describing my child. My kid can't tie his shoes". Or, "They fall on their head for literally no reason. There's not that much going on up there yet". A child may not have grasp of certain, specific tasks, but most of those involve underdeveloped coordination and motor skills, not cognitive deficiencies.

The human brain is an infinitely complex machine that I doubt science will ever fully understand. Your child came into this world breathing, feeling, wanting, needing, and screaming at the top of their lungs. It's incredible the amount of information the human brain processes at an early age. In fact, infancy to childhood is the time their little brains grow the fastest.

Understand when formulating responses, you should only give the measured answer their mind needs to their specific questions. This helps their mind process and protect its self. This method will help them grow while you foster the safety they'll need when it's time to ask more difficult questions in the future.

It bears repeating that the process can grow more complicated by telling a child's siblings more than they themselves know. Don't discount the possibility relatives, friends, and others can provide children with more information than they've asked for. This is the exact reason it's important to ensure everyone's on the same page where the release of information and who provides it, are concerned. If everyone directs your child back to you and if you listen to the exact questions they ask, there's no reason you can't avoid this pitfall.

TELLING BEFORE THEY'RE READY

Another all too common pitfall takes place when caregivers tell their child the entire story of their absentee parent before they're ready. As with all pitfalls, this should be avoided at all costs.

This pitfall differs from the others in that parents, who tell their child before their ready, set out to commit this pitfall from the child's earliest age and for very different purposes than forcing the issue, which follows the parent's arbitrary schedule.

It's all too common. I speak with parent's who respond in one of two ways to the question, "What's the last question your child asked about their absentee parent?"

The first response is one of satisfaction. "My child doesn't ask anything. I told them the whole story before they could talk and continued to tell them until they didn't ask anymore. They know the whole story."

The second is one of frustration. "I told my child the whole story several times, but they still ask one little question at a time. When they do, I give them the whole story, but they still ask questions." I feel bad for the children in either case.

I disagree with the school of thought that believes in telling a child everything before their crystallized memory develops. Once they're told, the parent continues to rinse and repeat, knowing their child will have knowledge of the situation from their earliest memories. They point to the case of adopted children who're told from early childhood they were adopted, so it doesn't come as a surprise in later years.

There's a noticeable difference between these examples. A child, adopted into an intact, two parent household, would have no reason to ask if they were adopted. The child with an absentee parent is born into very different circumstances. They easily see differences between the households of their classmates and friends and their own. They know there are questions to be asked, and believe me, they will.

The exception to this rule is the child whose single parent or guardian has either remarried or had the same significant-other since before their child entered grade school. Before this point, a child has recollections of only five to ten memories. Chances are very slim that one of these memories will be of the parents wedding or the partner moving in.

In these cases, it might be appropriate to remind a child three to four times a year that the parent's happy to discuss the absentee parent whenever they want. This allows a child to have memories that there is a person they may need information about in the future. This method (in this specific situation) also opens the channels of communication for the child and directs them to come to their parent when they're ready to ask questions.

With that scenario discussed, it's self serving to place the entire story of the absentee parent on the shoulders of a child, too young to make determinations about the information they receive. Understanding, as you do at this point, how a child's mind works and how they ask questions regarding the absentee parent, it's not in the child's best interest to hear the entire story from an early age. This begs the question, who does it benefit?

In many cases a parent feels a need to either confide in another, as a client would with a therapist, or craft their own version of history that's difficult to shake or contradict in later years. Either is inappropriate for its own reasons.

It's imperative not to allow a child to act as free mental counsel. It may make the caregiver feel better at the moment, but treating

97

a child as you would a trusted, adult confidant causes so much more harm for the child than good. I've heard countless stories of parents confiding in their child the most intimate details of their life, especially those dealing with the pain caused by an absentee parent. Trust me, the parent's cathartic release today will cost so much more in therapy fees for the child, down the road.

The other reason some tell their child before they're ready is to shape a story in early childhood so engrained, the child won't question it. This option seems quite a bit like brainwashing, with good reason. No one wants to lead and teach their child through subversion.

I take that back, some do. But those individuals refuse to read books like this. That being said, I have faith this pitfall is either unintentional or well meaning, although misguided, in the majority of caregivers who find they engage in this practice.

In short, follow the plan. Tell children what they want to know, when they want to know it, not before. A parent should avoid the urge to tell their child anything at an early age with the aim of making the parent feel better. As you know, the focus is the child and what's best for them.

As said before, tell a child when they're ready, in their time. It may feel better for the parent to get the story off their chest all at once. I'm certain that's the case. But remembering the effect it could have on a child, the story in its entirety is probably better told to a therapist, minister, or close friend. There's no shame in talking to someone about your feelings and thoughts. It's one of the best steps a parent can take to move beyond the absentee parent and the pain they caused and return to the normalcy of life. So long as a parent ensures the person receiving the information dump isn't their child.

Beyond the issues of giving the child too much information, a parent can cause a strange dynamic shift to take place where the child is given power they don't deserve to have at such an early age. This can also affect the child's relationships with other adults, going forward. Instead, it's a good rule of thumb to exclude a child from any discussions that feel more like therapy or friends talking, than a normal conversation with healthy parent/child boundaries.

Approach every situation concerning the absentee parent as a means to give your child the answers they request, nothing more. If they feel comfortable enough to ask for information in chunks, answer in the same manner.

The frequency of questions will accelerate in years to come and you'll long for the time when they asked questions like, "Do I have a mama?" or "Why doesn't Daddy live with us?" In the future, usually during their late teens or early twenties, you'll find yourself sitting down for two or three very long conversations about your child's absentee parent, but as in earlier chapters, let them guide the flow and direction of information.

They'll thank you as adults, not just for allowing them to have the childhood they deserve, but also for giving them the opportunity to come to you to discuss any subject, at any time. Your attitude about absentee parent questions will affect your child's comfort level discussing any matters important to them. This comfort will make the teenage years and the transition into adulthood so much easier. It's amazing that this level of closeness and comfort can be fostered through such difficult questions asked in childhood; the same ones that otherwise cause so much stress.

BEING OVERLY CRITICAL

Other pitfalls may be as frequent but none are as difficult to quell as a parents temptation to be overly critical of the absentee parent. Let's face the facts, for whatever reason the absentee parent isn't there for parent or child, hence the term "absentee". They aren't doing something others probably feel, with good reason, they should.

Whatever issues a parent has with the absentee parent are probably justified, but those issues are between the parent and absentee parent. Nothing's gained from subjecting a child to these issues. Little ones don't understand the inner workings and complexities of adult relationships. They shouldn't have to. They won't understand the relationship between their parent and their absentee parent and that's healthy. An in depth understanding of adult relationships could show a level of crossed boundaries and enmeshment that borders on toxic.

I understand the temptation to be overly critical. Interestingly a large portion of those interviewed felt they weren't being critical at all. This is a point to take note of. They give responses like, "I'm just telling them what happened.", or "I'm just telling it like it really was". In reality it's entirely too easy to fall into this pitfall and it's surprising to most what's considered overly critical.

I'll give a couple of examples of what could be considered overly critical:

> Son: Mommy, why isn't Daddy here?
>
> Mother: I don't know, baby. He just left. That's what he does.

In this example, it would've been just as easy to say, "I don't know, baby". Anything more in this case is unnecessary. Everything else is overly critical. In fact, this pitfall stems, in part, from a lack of attention to the two moment rule. If a parent takes one moment to consider what's asked, and the crucial second moment to strip away all emotion from the answer, they decrease radically the chance they'll commit this pitfall.

It's important to note there are invariably three sides to every story: your version, their version, and the facts. Stick to the facts. Avoid emotion. "I don't know" does work if you truly don't know. Be careful answering too many questions with this response. Using the answer, "I don't know" for every question could either trigger more questions, or lead the child to feel their parent is being avoidant. If the latter occurs, the child will stop asking questions.

In situations like this, it might be more advisable to answer the question "Why isn't Daddy here?" along these lines. "Daddy isn't here because he lives somewhere else".

As said before, give them a hug and say, "I love you. Is there anything else you want to ask?" Some answer is better than no answer, however, sometimes a different wording of, "I don't know", might make all the difference.

I realize a mental red flag might go up for most parents or guardians either having to deal with an absentee parent or those who have a history with them. You might think, "Yeah, but my child would just ask another question". Those parents are probably right. That seems logical.

Kids love to play, "The Why Game". Most parents can recount stories of scouring the internet to figure out, for their child, why a jelly fish stings or what a Muppet is actually made of. It's amazing though, how often a child doesn't ask another question. The fear is that a child will hit us with a battery of questions. My surveys and interviews haven't shown this to be the case.

When I look at the actual interactions between parents or guardians and their children, I've found in most cases, children ask one to three questions, nothing more. What happens if they do? What if your child asks another question?

If your child asks more questions, that's wonderful. That's what you want. Take it as the good sign it is. It shows your child's clarifying their questions. More questions show they're comfortable with you. It shows you're doing something right. That being said don't mistake one question for a lack of communication and try to force the issue. Allow them to be where they are. When you're hit with a bevy of questions make sure you don't fall off the tracks and possibly bring communication to a stop.

What I mean by this is that it'd be possible to do exactly what I'm asking; to give only the information they're asking... for a question or two. When some parents are hit with the third or forth question, one of three things might happen: Hopefully you stay the course and continue with what's working. However, it's also possible for a parent to become frazzled by the onslaught of questions and forget the method. It's also common in some parents to become comfortable with their child and decide they can handle more information. Resist the urge. Continue assessing what your child asks and only answer the exact wording you hear. While doing so, don't forget to enjoy these interactions with your child. These are the moments that'll bring you closer, depending, of course, how they're handled. Here's another example:

Daughter: Daddy, why doesn't Mama call on my birthday?

Father: It's ok. I'm here. I forgot to call and remind her. She probably doesn't remember.

His response has several issues. Although each sentence is a common response from a loving parent, each should be avoided. In this case, the father did well to remind his child he's there for her and he loves her.

However, there's a glaring issue with the first sentence. The response, "It's Ok, I'm here", completely ignores the actual question his child asked, making her feel her Dad's either too uncomfortable with the subject, or simply being avoidant.

Beyond that thought, other forces are at work in this statement. The father goes on to say, "I forgot to call and remind her". In doing so, he unknowingly sets himself up as the villain or bad guy.

It's true you shouldn't be overly critical of the absentee parent. However, there's also no need to vilify yourself. Don't throw yourself under the bus and be overly critical of yourself for the sake of saving the absentee parents image. This can be equally harmful, causing unnecessary issues between parent and child. This by the way, is such a common issue, it warrants its own separate pitfall chapter.

The final statement, "She probably didn't remember." is also problematic. The father doesn't know whether the parent forgot, chose not to call or had something happen. It's better to minimize the amount of information and err on the side of caution.

A better response to the question "Daddy, why doesn't Mama call on my birthday?" is as simple as, "I don't know, baby. I love you". It should put your mind at ease to know some questions just don't have answers. If the answer to a question truly is "I don't know," there's no shame in that response. So long as it doesn't become a habit or a means of avoidance, your child will accept the occasional, I don't know. I can honestly say my child has asked questions I didn't know the answer to and I was quick to say I didn't know. If your child presses, they'll do so by changing the wording of their question. This allows you to answer a different question all together.

This theme has been repeated in virtually every chapter, but it bears repeating. Above all else, show your child you love them. Remind them none of this is their fault. Then reassure them it's ok to come to you with problems and questions. Those three steps will help your child through any and every difficult time.

Some ask what problem there could possibly be painting the absentee parent as the villain they are. If they were concerned about what's said, they'd be here. They aren't alone.

The act of being overly critical of an absentee parent is exceedingly common. There are two issues to consider, however 1. As distasteful as it may seem now, the absentee parent is still just that, the child's parent (absent though they may be). 2. As harsh as it is, any failings in the relationship are irrelevant at this point. It doesn't matter whether the absentee parent's a former spouse or significant other. The sole focus is the child and their needs.

Caregiver's who paint the absentee parent as a monster cause their children to defend the parent who isn't there. This makes them defenseless in the child's eyes. The less parents succumb to this desire, the more they minimize this protective need in their child.

This is especially important for the person who performs all the daily duties of the absentee parent, without the gift of genetic relation. This could include a spouse or significant other, a relative or family friend. Anyone in this caption should take extra care to ensure they don't engage in this activity. I say this because of the added frustration this form of parent can feel, when the child they do everything for, asks about the person who isn't there for them.

Being overly critical of the absentee parent is such an easy thing to do. It can be instantaneous, almost automatic, but resist the urge. No one wants to put their child in a position where they feel forced to defend their absentee parent. The caregiver who spends their time being overly critical of the absentee parent stands the very real possibility of driving their child away at a speed few other actions can.

Releasing the emotion of a past relationship or parent's absence is a start in the direction of balanced answers to questions your child might ask. Just take your two moments before you answer. Focus on the exact wording of the question, strip the emotion from your response and you'll do just fine.

SUGAR COATING
OR CREATING MARTYRS

Some are so aware of the pitfall mentioned in the last chapter; they go overboard avoiding the mistake. This can be just as damaging as being overly critical of the absentee parent, although this pitfall is not as common. Some parents tend to sugar coat the story of the absentee parent or martyr themselves or others while answering absentee parent questions. I realize how difficult this information has to feel at the moment. Don't be overly critical – don't sugar coat. Which is it?

Unfortunately, where absentee parent discussions are concerned, it's a tightrope act. You have to take care not to commit either pitfall. Thankfully, the key to successfully avoiding many of these pitfalls is to know the pitfalls, take your two moments and answer exactly what's asked, while showing your child you love them.

People who commit the hazard of sugar coating or creating martyrs minimize the absentee parent's lack of involvement in the child's life. Most are concerned about the child's relationship with the absentee parent, in the event the absentee parent does return.

Admittedly this pitfall is mainly committed by grandparents, hoping for the best in their absentee parent/ child. While it's wonderful to hold optimistic expectations for an absentee parent, there's often more damage caused than the intended goodwill the caregiver hopes to foster.

I realize some ask what it hurts to paint the absentee parent in a positive light. Vilification and canonization are equally problematic. Painting the absentee parent in an inappropriately favorable light is harmful and here's why. In the absence of someone to blame, the absentee parent in this situation find themselves beyond reproach in the mind of their child.

How exactly will that affect the child? Painting the absentee parent in an inappropriately positive light causes the child to question who made the absentee parent leave, since the absentee parent themselves wouldn't do such a thing. In a way, sugar coating makes the absentee parent a hero and where there's a hero, there has to be a villain.

In the absence of someone else to blame, the parent, guardian, significant other or the child themselves will take the mantle as the reason for the absentee parents' departure.

The child in this case is much more likely to seek out the hero in later years. This only sets them up for further disappointment when the absentee parent turns out to be a fallible human being, as everyone is. This pitfall can be avoided by dealing only in the requested facts. Doing otherwise is very similar to the next pitfall, lying.

Will your child still make these assumptions? There's always a chance they'll question their involvement in their absentee parent's exodus. This in small measure is normal. However the positive, loving reinforcement and reassurance you provide will be your child's saving grace in those difficult times of self questioning.

It's equally troubling for a child whose parent or guardian positions them self as a saint, completely free from blame or reproach. This only sets the parent up for failure. Parents sometimes do this to place themselves above the circumstances or choices that bought them to the point of single parenthood.

Some parents do so out of fear their child will have no one else to look up to. In these cases they manufacture a better version of themselves for their child's sake. Doing so forces the parent to walk the talk for the rest of their lives, without relapse into their former, normal selves. This causes issues, as perfection proves to be too much pressure. Eventually the parent's old self resurfaces, causing their child to question the facade they've been told to believe their entire childhood.

To avoid such issues, I represent myself as a fallible human being who constantly makes little mistakes. I use these moments to show my son that mistakes are necessary to make improvements. I teach him that mistakes are important so long as you learn from them. From what I've seen, he doesn't seem to love me any less for allowing him to see my less than perfect self.

Children whose parents place themselves above the fray, almost certainly believe the unreasonable claims, until some event or action knocks them off the proverbial pedestal. When this does happen, the parent has a long fall in their child's eyes.

Parents who place themselves on a pedestal also present their child with a different issue, in addition to the impending plunge. Such maneuvering places the child in an impossible situation. They can't compete with, or live up to the impossible standard the parent has manufactured. This can manifest as issues, even years later, in the form of failed relationships, difficulties at work, and a myriad of other problems. It should also be noted, parents on pedestals set themselves apart from their children, making it impossible to be emotionally close or share open communication. The distance, even standing side by side, is just too great to overcome. Where as the parent who shows their child the productive side of mistakes, avoids these issues.

I'm reminded of a situation where a father positioned himself as a modern day Lance-a-lot to his children and everyone else in his community. He could do no wrong and was above the mistakes of common people, including those of his own children.

The imagery turned out to be more poignant than he knew. Amidst all his bolstering and narcissism the father hid a serious flaw in his character. Years later this flaw manifested itself in a less than acceptable way, which caused a great deal of disbelief and pain for everyone involved. Even though his children were grown at the time of the scandal, the incident shook them to their very foundations, causing each of his now grown children issues in different areas of their lives.

We're all human. We all make mistakes. It's best to be transparent and allow your child to see the flawed side of you as well and I make that statement very carefully. I'm not in any way advocating the promotion of illegal, unethical, or immoral behavior to children. The statement is not meant as a get out of jail free card for a parent to involve their child in vices, secrets, or inappropriate behavior.

What I am saying is to allow your child to see your imperfect side, the side that makes common, everyday mistakes. Let them see the person who forgot to put oil in the lawn mower before starting it or the person who left the Thanksgiving turkey on the table with the dog in the house. Let them know that sometimes you forget to lock the door behind you or that maybe you made an error at work that you had to make up for.

These occasional moments provide amazing teaching opportunities and give your child realistic examples of a person they can not only be proud of, but can easily relate to. Not to mention a person who can relate to them in their times of need.

Your life will be all the more stress free and you'll find they'll only love you more for it. So avoid the pitfall of sugar coating or martyring people when discussing an absentee parent and know they'll love you more for who you are, than who you pretend to be, warts and all.

LYING

Last but certainly not least on the list of pitfalls to avoid is lying. Don't do it. There is only rarely, if ever, a reason to lie to your child concerning an absentee parent. A good example would be, if their absentee parent is a child abuser or some other form of convicted felon (and I only use those examples very seriously and sparingly). Although even in these situations there's no need to lie, but rather choose words carefully.

Even these questions are easily answered. Although I realize it's always a fear someone in this situation lives with, what are the chances a child will come to a parent and ask, "Is Daddy a child molester?" or, "How many people has Mommy killed?" I can assure you it's a rarity.

Children ask questions and those questions should be answered truthfully. Eventually the child will start honing their questions based on the factual responses a parent or guardian gives. That's to be expected. More difficult questions still require loving, caring, factual answers. Answer questions in a way that fosters the feeling in a child that they're not to blame and that they're a good person who's loved.

What if a child does come to their parent at an early age and asks a very specific, damaging question about their absentee parent? Answer truthfully and understand children don't come up with damning questions without help. This would point to someone feeding the child a question or making a statement that causes the question to be asked, as a matter of clarification. The worst thing to do in this case is lie.

Lying about an absentee parent will always come back to haunt you. Children eventually find out and the relationship with their parent will be fractured from that moment forward. Lying about the answer to one question regarding an absentee parent could easily cause the child to question every statement the parent ever made. It's always better to be truthful.

It's also important though to ascertain exactly where the child received the information that provided the basis for their question. The person who fed the child inappropriate information should then be made aware of the plan. Any information about the absentee parent comes from the parent and no one else.

The person who gives a child inappropriate information at an early age will likely not understand the damage these actions cause, without a serious, frank discussion. When it comes to questions about the absentee parent, make your expectations very clear to others.

An interesting manifestation of this pitfall occurs occasionally in stable families that move on, in the wake of an absentee parent's departure. Especially in cases where the child is still relatively young when the parent or guardian takes another spouse or significant other. There's a very real desire to write the absentee parent completely out of the picture and allow the child to believe they were conceived within the nuclear family that now exists.

While this seems like a good idea for those considering it, I would advise against any such action. I myself am a person in this situation and I can tell you my child, at this point, has no memory of life before my wife. She is the perfect, loving parent for him in every way I can imagine. But even with all this in mind, we've still been very upfront with him, allowing for open honest communication about his absentee parent. For example, we have a wedding picture, featuring my son, prominently displayed where he can see it.

I realize there may be painful memories to contend with, especially once the parent moves on and sees how life without the absentee parent can be. But this pain doesn't compare to the sense of betrayal a child feels when someday such a story is exposed. It might seem easier at the time to do otherwise, but I can tell you without exception, this plan backfires with grave consequences, as we'll see in the following examples.

An interesting manifestation of this pitfall would be a mother who isn't certain of her child's biological father. I say the mother only because there'll always be a birth certificate somewhere with the mothers name on it. Not to mention a father or grandparent wouldn't accept delivery of a child without receiving at least some clarifying information about the absentee mother.

There's never any way to know if and how things may unfold in the future, so it's best, even in these cases, not to lie to the child. If the mother has a best guess scenario, it would be ok to give that persons information and include the phrase, "I believe", or to even say I'm not sure.

This brings us to another aspect of the lying pitfall. Never tell a child outlandish lies about their absentee parent. No matter how tempting it may be, avoid the temptation. It would be easy, especially in times of war, to claim a child's parent was killed while performing some act of bravery or that they were involved in some positive situation that ended in their untimely demise.

A real world example of this I've encountered was that of a person who was told his father had been killed in action in Vietnam. In this case, the mother had a great deal of personal information about the father.

Upon entering college, the boy decided to seek out his father's medals and his paternal grandparents, so he could hear more about this wonderful man he'd never known. The name of the man he'd been given had served in Vietnam in the 1960's, however he'd died seven years before the boys birth. Furthermore, the man's parents relayed that he'd never been to the boy's birth state. To add to the mystery, the boy realized in college he was actually born two years after the end of the Vietnam War era.

When confronted, his mother told him she only happened to select a name that belonged to a serviceman killed in action in Vietnam. She'd been a "wild child" in her early days and wasn't sure who his father was. It could have been one of three people. One died while drunk driving several years earlier and the other two had spent several years in prison on armed robbery charges.

She wanted him to have a father he could be proud of but instead, he felt his entire life had been built on a lie.

This boy had been humiliated in front of the U.S. government and the parents of this poor deceased stranger. After he and his mother had their initial confrontation over her handling of the situation, he ceased contact with her. The cover up of a difficult time in her early adulthood ultimately led to her exclusion from the boy's life. This is an extreme example, but I fear a common one.

Another example involves a young boy who constantly changed stories of his fathers' occupation and why he wasn't around. Many thought the boy was fabricating a father for himself. After closer examination however, it became evident the boy's mother was the problem. She didn't remember from day to day the wonderful stories she'd told about his absentee father.

In this child's case, his father had an affair with the boy's mother. The boy had known his father his entire life, only he knew him as the nice man a few doors down who always included him on family outings.

It wasn't until years later he picked up a picture of the nice neighbor man as a child and noticed the surprising similarities to his own baby pictures. At the time, both relationships faced almost insurmountable trust issues.

These two examples are not intended to imply this only happens to women or that men don't commit the same mistakes. They do. A real example involving a father quickly comes to mind.

This father was upset his ex wife had left him and his young son for a man in another part of the country. He concocted a story about her drinking too much at a party. She had, in his story, decided to drive home against everyone's wishes and wrecked, sustaining injuries and ultimately dying.

The father told his son the story so he wouldn't feel abandoned. He felt safe in lying to his son because he had assurances the ex wife wouldn't return. Truth be told, he mostly told his son out of anger that he'd been left to raise the little boy on his own.

He expected his wife would keep her promise. He didn't expect the boy to search out his maternal grandparents to hear about his mothers redeeming qualities. Of course, the boy did find his grandparents, who promptly showed him recent pictures of his mother and siblings. They relayed the story as they were told by the mother. In that moment, both the father's lies and the boy's life unraveled. The boy, not trusting his father, sought his mother and asked to start a new life with her.

It's important to remember, no matter how absent a parent might be, or for that matter promises to be, they're still in the picture, by virtue of the possibility they'll resurface at some point. I'd advise against anyone telling a child they don't have a mother or father, unless the absentee parent is actually deceased and you've personally seen the burial plot or confirmed with reliable sources they have in fact passed away.

Of course, if that's the case you need a different book that covers grief and related issues. The parent who relays to a child they only have one parent stands a very real risk. The parent, who showed no interest over the first several years of the child's life, could suddenly reemerge, wanting to rekindle old relationships.

The child who receives only facts will be much better prepared for this eventuality than one who believes no other parent exists. So take your two moments, state only truthful facts regarding the absentee parent, and let the child know they're loved.

There is a moral to these stories. Telling the truth would've avoided these familial problems later in life. Don't mistake this pitfall to mean the children in these scenarios needed all absentee parent information from early childhood. Doing so would be committing a pitfall listed earlier.

When the children in these cases asked their questions, the parents should've weighed the question, taking into account only the exact, emotion free facts. They then could've answered the child's question, while letting them know they're loved, adding that the child is not to blame.

The children in these examples would've asked small questions at first and then continued through childhood and adolescence, slowly asking more difficult questions as time went on. This makes the process of telling the child the truth much more palatable. Leading a child down a path that brings them to the truth is difficult, but necessary. Following the steps set forth in earlier chapters will help bring parent and child closer in the process.

HELPING MY CHILD

Of course, there's never a way to say with complete certainty a child will not find themselves in the same position later in life. There's nothing in my background that would suggest I'd be having this discussion with my son today.

All we can do is raise our kids as best we can. We'll send them out into the world after high school or college and hope we taught them right. That being said, there are some things you can do during childhood to improve their chances of avoiding this same set of circumstances.

Surrounding a child with people who maintain and model authentic, healthy relationships is one of the most basic actions you can take for your child. This subconsciously gives them a schematic to navigate when they enter the world of intimate relationships, later in life. It doesn't matter whether these people are your parents, a couple you work with or the cute, elderly couple in the first pew during the early service. Surround your child with happy, committed couples. Don't be afraid to draw attention to positive relationships around them.

Discuss the positive attributes of these relationships, but never do so at the expense of your current situation. While it's a good idea to point out exceptional couples around you, never draw comparisons between these couples and your current family situation, whatever that may be.

Your child is in the best situation they can be in because they're with you. You care deeply about them and you keep them safe. Avoid scenarios where your child might see their current circumstances as inferior or less than optimal. There's no reason to draw connections that don't exist. Doing so can harm your relationship with your child. It can even harm their vision and memory of their own childhood, compared to others.

For this same reason, avoid painting yourself as an ineffective or substandard parent. Keep clear in your mind the difference between applauding the successful relationships of others and sabotaging your own effectiveness as a parent.

Another factor that will have some impact on your child's future is your relationship with them. Of course, the guidelines discussed in this book should assist you. It's important to be a person your child can come to, with questions or issues they may have in any area of their life. Let yourself be the person they can talk to and they will. The old adage is correct – communication is key.

Another great way to improve your child's chances of having fulfilling, committed relationships is to surround them with a supportive network of family, friends, social groups and religious affiliations. The more happy, non toxic interactions a child can have with trusted adults, the better. Keep them around positive members of the family, especially those willing to follow the guidelines you set for absentee parent discussions.

I feel I should preface this next suggestion with a disclaimer. I'm not stating that any person is at a disadvantage if they are opposed to following any of this advice. I am however saying there's evidence to support community inclusion as a predictor of a child's success.

That being said, some fear the prospect of taking their child into a church, sighting the way they have been or might be treated as a single parent. There's a good chance you will run into a couple of people in any social or religious setting who'll be condescending or judgmental about your situation, but even those people provide teachable moments. You can have a discussion with your child about the way to act, or not act as the case may be.

I've found in my own church experience that everyone was much more supportive than I ever thought possible. The majority of people want to help. They want a child to be raised in a community, where they can be watched and protected by the trusted multitude.

I'm not in any way suggesting you have to subscribe to any specific form of religion or that you have to take your child to church. What I am saying is that having your child in a positive community environment, of any type, is extremely beneficial to their later success.

Another good outlet that promotes positive interactions is extra curricular activities. Having your child in any form of team activity will help them relationally in the future. In addition to team activities like sports, dance, acting, and martial arts, individual activities like music lessons, meditation and exercise also help children significantly, especially if you engage in the process in a positive way with them. Music, meditation and exercise teach children motivation and determination, alongside ideals of peaceful resolution, accomplishment and the value of goal directed work.

Another mediating factor in a child's success may sound silly, but it turns out to be exceedingly important. Eat meals with your child. Several studies have found higher levels of success in children who ate several meals per week, at a table, with their immediate family. Doing so allows a parent to ask about their child's day. It's usually at this time, children talk about any problems they're having.

Ask open ended questions that require more in depth answers than the usual yes or no. Take the opportunity to tell them how you're doing. It can be a little difficult if you start during their teenage years, but a child who's accustomed to nightly family dinner doesn't question the ritual. If your work schedule allows, it's worth the investment and if you're lucky, maybe they'll start learning how to wash the dishes.

Along the same lines as family dinner, another seemingly extraneous predictor of success in children is bedtime stories. If your child's still young enough, read them a bedtime story when you tuck them in at night. This gives more bonding time with your little one. It also provides parents a bit of stress relief. If your child is a little too old to be read to (for those with tweeners and teenagers) take the same time every night before they go to bed.

Pick a subject that interests the two of you and read up on it to have nightly discussions. Perhaps you can take turns reading the latest People or Entertainment Weekly magazine. Maybe you can each talk about a favorite sports team or sports magazine. Try to pick something you agree on, for the most part. You don't want every night to be a fight. Enjoy your time together bonding over common interests.

While the ideas mentioned above are known to enhance child development, the activities mentioned below do just the opposite, causing in most cases turmoil for the children involved.

Parading a host of people in and out of the child's life tops the list of predictors against success. Doing so opens the child to a distorted view of healthy relationships. There was a study done a couple of years ago that sited a strong correlation between the number of live-in relationships a custodial single parent has and the extent to which a child displays conduct disorder tendencies. In layman's terms this means a whole lot of meetings with the principal and in school suspensions in the child's future, not to mention potential prison time.

This environment also increases the likelihood a child will be harmed. The more overnight visitors and loose relational guests move in and out of the child's life, the more likely they are to be abused in some form or fashion by one or more of these people.

I remember meeting a child who had so many Daddy Jack's and Daddy Mark's and Daddy insert names here, they had an inappropriate view of what a father was. What their role in the family was, and what they were allowed and not allowed to do. There's no reason to chance this with any little one.

Realizing it's necessary for people to have adult time and seek healthy adult relationships, it might be good to exchange sleep over nights for the kids with someone you trust, who's in your position. This removes the child from a potentially harmful and detrimental environment. Especially since, as one of my friends would say, "Your picker's broken or you wouldn't be here".

I say this of course jokingly, but I think there's some truth in it. As single parents, we've made mistakes in the past regarding who we've chosen. This increases our chances of repeating past transgressions, unless we do some personal work and get our picker fixed.

Of course, grandparents and family friends placed in a parenting role by the absence of a biological parent may not have broken pickers. If your picker's working fine, don't change a thing. For the rest of us there's no time like the present to examine those former patterns. However, that subject requires a different book.

One thing I've done with my little one to curb poor decision making in his future was to discuss decision making while he was still preschool age. We had, and continue to have, talks about how decisions can affect us for a long time and how these decisions have lasting consequences, both good and bad.

I'd advise against ever even hinting at the possibility your child is a mistake or in some way a poor decision. This again is a process of separating the child from the absentee parent. Your personal opinion of the absentee parent, I would hope, is very different from your feelings for your child.

Make certain not to confuse the two while talking to your child. Doing so will have lasting negative effects. In fact, I would completely erase the phrase, "Don't make the same mistakes I did," from your vocabulary. It never fails to elicit visions in the child's mind that you are calling them a mistake, which couldn't be further from the truth. There's no good way to paint yourself out of that corner, so avoid the phrase all together.

You can prepare them for a great future by asking questions now. I once asked my little one what he wanted to do when he grows up. When he responded, an astronaut, we discussed the different steps a person takes to become an astronaut. He and I researched the process together on the internet. We talked about the education and training necessary to become an astronaut. The discussion gave me a chance to talk to him about the importance of math and science. We took him to a day camp at the Johnson Space Center in Houston, where he got to play astronaut and make rockets for a day.

It's great to help your child focus. It's important though to be flexible enough to change with their ever changing mind. There's nothing wrong with a child who decides to look in a new direction, in fact it's healthy.

There are children who know they want to be veterinarians before they turn seven, that however is not the norm. Whatever your child's interest, take an interest in it yourself. The process will bring you closer. It will set the foundation for a lasting, healthy relationship, and the activity will allow you to flag potentially dangerous activities and friends before they become more difficult to curb.

Another discussion my little one and I have on a regular basis, I refer to as, "The Timeline Talk". It's good to set up a timeline you and your child can refer to, whatever their goals. Of course, this will look different for every parent/child relationship but in our case, whenever he mentions becoming a daddy, which is one of his main goals at the moment, I always respond, "I love being your Daddy and I think you'd make a great one – some day. What do you have to do before you can become a daddy?"

He always answers the question while counting off the steps on his fingers, "First I have to finish high school, then college, then

I can get my Masters, then I marry a really great girl who cares about me and treats me good. We buy a house and then we can have kids together".

He has that six step timeline he can rattle off anytime he talks about being a daddy or accomplishing anything. I'm not a parent who demands their child become a doctor or lawyer. My only demand is that he be happy. I'm pursuing my doctorate because it makes me happy and its work I enjoy. Whether he enjoys teaching elementary school, working on cars or becoming an astronaut, I'll be happy.

Whatever it is he decides to do, he has a timeline in mind that includes an education and notes that he needs to marry someone who loves him and cares about him. Talking to your child about the decisions they have to make in later life will help them consider the future and choose wisely. Telling them how great extra education is and talking to them about waiting to start a family helps children see they're capable of doing something great and that waiting to have a family is not necessarily a bad thing.

This type of method works on children in both directions. Children internalize everything they're told, both good and bad. Why not supply them with an array of wonderful, affirming statements that will motivate and help them to achieve their goals, instead of telling them they're not smart enough or that they can't do things. Start off early and tell them often how much you love them, how special and amazing they are, and how much faith you have in them. It sure beats the alternative. In most cases if you believe in your child, they'll believe in themselves. That can help them make good choices in bad times.

WHAT ELSE SHOULD I KNOW?

The first thing you need to know is that you're a great parent and you have what it takes to make it through this time that has potential to be extremely tough. Raising the children of absentee parents is becoming an increasingly common issue in today's society. It's estimated over half of all kids in the United States will be raised by single parents at some point during their childhood or adolescence. What does this mean for you? You're not alone. There are resources for single parents and the list is increasing every month.

I know you love your child. If you didn't, you never would've picked up this book, let alone read to the end. Show them you love them. Tell them how much you care about them and they'll respond. I have a child who resists those kinds of messages. I tell him I love him or that I think he's special and he just says, "Oh Dad".

However even if they act like it doesn't matter – it does. Children crave positive attention. They want your interaction with them and there's nothing wrong with giving as much as you possibly can.

Remember to be positive and optimistic towards them. Make sure you don't fall into the rut of only giving feedback when they're doing wrong. Catch them doing something right and compliment them for it. They'll appreciate that you notice and they'll love the positive attention.

I once heard Shane Lopez, the famous positive psychologist say, "It takes seven positive statements to overcome just one negative statement". Think about the number of positive things you say in comparison to the negative ones they hear. Be sure the message you send is in at least that ratio of 7 to 1. The outcome will amaze you.

The only other thing I suggest is to seek out therapy, for them, for you, and as a family. Thankfully therapy is becoming increasingly accepted in society. There's nothing wrong with letting another set of ears hear what you have to say. The act of going to therapy is stress relieving for most, eventually. It's also serves to show your child that it's ok to seek help. It's good to have an impartial third party relay their thoughts about a situation and it's always a good idea to work on communication.

If you prefer not to speak to a formal therapist, you can achieve similar results by speaking to a minister or trusted friend. What's more important than the persons title is that they listen and relay to you their view of the events, free from judgment and partiality.

CONCLUSION

I give you my most heartfelt congratulations for completing this book. I hope it's been helpful for you. If you know others who would benefit from this book or are struggling with similar issues, please feel free to pass this on or get them a copy.

As a matter of summing up what we've learned here, I hope you've gained better confidence about what to do when your child asks about their absentee parent. I hope you understand why the steps are so important. I further hope you take with you the idea of allowing two extra moments to pause after someone asks you a question: one to examine exactly what they've actually asked and one to strip the emotion from your response. This will help in many facets of your life, even beyond this subject matter.

I hope you see how the seven pitfalls of blaming, forcing, telling too much, telling too early, being critical, sugar coating, and lying can ruin your relationship with your child and cause them issues that'll be difficult, at best, to overcome. I trust you have the tools and knowledge to avoid these pitfalls when the possibility presents itself.

I feel it's important to note that this is an evolving process between you and your child. I want you to use what works, and abandon what doesn't fit your situation. No one knows your kiddo better than you, so use your intuition and continually think about and question yourself on ways you can improve your relationship with your child.

No matter how good a relationship is, it can always improve through better communication. I hope you keep that in the back of your mind when dealing with your little one. Communication is key.

This book represents a guideline of the plan I use with my own child, the plan that works and has worked well for us. Adapt it and change it as needed to make it work for you and your child. I'm very interested to hear your successes, your challenges, your questions and suggestions for future editions.

Please feel free to leave any feedback and take part in online forums at http://www.AbsenteeParentBook.com. I want to hear from you and I wish you the very best in this journey you and your child have embarked on. I have complete faith in you and your ability to discuss with your child the parent who's no longer there.

APPENDIX A
THE PROCESS

Small snippets from each chapter have been compiled in this quick reference guide. While this sheet shouldn't take the place of the text, it can act as a helpful reminder of general ideas from the book. It's advised to go back through the book from time to time as a refresher to ensure you have the plan clear in your mind. However, this quick reference guide will hopefully serve to keep this plan fresh without the need to constantly read and reread.

What's the process?

Remember the two moment approach. 1. Internalize the exact wording they use. 2. Strip all emotion from your response. Ask your child if they have any other questions. Praise them for coming to you. Remind them you love them.

What exactly should I tell them?

Answer what they ask. Nothing less. Nothing more.

When do I tell them?

Tell them only what they ask, when they ask. Follow their schedule rather than your own.

How do I tell them?

Get down on their level. Look them in the eye. Follow the two moment approach.

Where should I tell them?

Tell them immediately, wherever they ask.

Don't put it off. Whether it's in the grocery store or in traffic, enjoy the opportunity to share with them and impart the knowledge and peace of mind they're requesting.

Why should I tell them?

If you don't, they'll hear it elsewhere or they'll make up their own version of events. Answer their questions and encourage them to ask more as a means of bringing the two of you closer and fostering an open relationship.

APPENDIX B
THE PITFALLS

1. Blaming the child

The situation's not their fault. Asking questions can be frightening. Keep in mind when answering their questions, if a parent shows anger, their child won't come to them in the future.

2. Force the issue

Don't give a child information they haven't requested. Let them approach you with their questions. Let them know they can come to you and they will.

3. Answering more than they ask

Avoid the urge. You'll have plenty of time. Let it come on their terms.

4. Telling too early

Tell them on their time schedule, not yours. Remember their minds only ask what they can emotionally handle.

5. Being overly critical

This causes the child to feel as though they have to defend the absentee parent. The child might assume they're bad in some way as well.

6. Sugar coating or making martyrs

Children are likely to blame their parents or themselves for the issues with the absentee parent. Don't martyr yourself either. It only sets a parent up for failure.

7. Lying

They'll find out and when they do, things will always be much worse. Tell the truth from the beginning to avoid this pitfall. Difficult as the facts may be to relive, having them come to life later, is a far more painful proposition for everyone involved.

APPENDIX C
RESOURCE GUIDE

In this day and age it's increasingly difficult to provide a comprehensive list of resources to readers. Websites close daily or change their addresses and links, making it almost certain any resource guide would be obsolete by book printing.

To curb this eventuality, a resource guide is posted on my website. I'll continue to update and expand as more resources become available. I don't intend this to be a static list, but rather a growing interactive process. That being said, feel free to share great resources you've found and let me know about entries you weren't impressed with. Your thoughts are important in helping others in our situation. Access your free, updated resource guide at: http://www.AbsenteeParentBook.com/Resources

ABOUT THE AUTHOR

At the time this book was written, Scott Luper was a single parent to his preschool aged son. During the final writing and editing process, he married his long time girlfriend Vanessa and the two started crafting a way to co-parent a child primarily raised by a single parent. He lives with his wife and sons in Fort Worth, Texas, where he completed a master degree in clinical psychology. Scott has served on the board of directors for the Texas Psychological Association as well as numerous volunteer and civic boards. "Absentee Parent/Left Behind Child" is his second book and his first single author project. He also coauthored the international bestseller, "Wake Up... Moments of Inspiration". For more information on Scott or to leave feedback, please log onto http://www.ScottLuper.com.

To invite Scott to speak or to find a workshop in your area, visit: http://www.AbsenteeParentBook.com/Workshop

WWW.ABSENTEEPARENTBOOK.COM

Made in the USA
Monee, IL
11 March 2021

62489611R00094